AT THE CROSSROADS
OF
IMAGINE WHAT IF

HOW THE PRAYERS OF THE PATRIARCHS, PROPHETS, AND KINGS
CAN IMPACT YOUR LIFE AND OUR NATION
FOR GOOD

LALLAH BRILHART

May this book cause you to fall more deeply in love with Jesus and His marvelous Word. May it ignite in you a passion for prayer.

Blessings,

Lallah Brilhart

Published by BookLocker.com, Inc., St. Petersburg, Florida.

Printed on acid-free paper.

BookLocker.com, Inc.
2017

First Edition

Scripture references are from the New International Bible, copyright 1983

Lovingly dedicated to
Pastors Lloyd and Gwenda Fuss,
my spiritual parents.
Many years ago they instilled in me
a passion for the Word of God;
a longing to come before His
Throne of Grace in prayer;
and a burning desire to seek the Presence
Of the One Who sits on that Throne,
Christ Jesus, my Savior and Lord.
I am forever grateful.

ACKNOWLEDGEMENTS

Many, many thanks to my best friend and covenant partner of 47 years, Walter Brilhart. He has inspired me, encouraged me, believed in me, been longsuffering and patient with me, and given me confidence to write this book. He is a model of a Christian man and husband.

Thank you to Pastor Robb Goodman of Zion Freedom Fellowship in Westminster, Maryland; Pastor Chester Jones of Calvary Bible Chapel in Alamosa, Colorado; dear friends Jennifer Leck of Frederick, Maryland and Amanda Sackett of Westminster, Maryland. These four planted the seed to write a book and continued to water it in the process.

Thank you to Pastors Lloyd and Gwenda Fuss, Pastors John and Charlene Holmes, Pastors Bill and Linda Thomas, Pastors Jack and Cheryl Adams, and Pastors Steve and Sherri Robbins for sewing into my life the Word of God.

Thank you to my adult Sunday School class at Hope Chapel in Westminster, Maryland, who allowed me to "practice" on them by sharing with them some of the teachings of this book.

Thank you to all my brothers and sisters in Christ who have walked this journey of life with me. A special thanks to those who prayed for this book, and who supported me in the process.

Thank you to Walter Brilhart, Kathy McCaffrey and Jennifer Leck, and Alaina Haerbig. They each spent many laborious hours editing this book. It was indeed a gift of love.

For those who might be interested, Alaina would like to offer her editing services. She may be reached at:

alainabeth2030@hotmail.com

Finally, and above all - praise, worship, adoration, and thanksgiving to Jesus Christ, my Lord and Savior, who rescued me from an empty life and filled me to overflowing with His Spirit. He has captured my heart forever.

FOREWORD

Having been raised in the Lutheran faith, Lallah always had a deep reverence for the Lord. There was something different about her the day we met. She had a personality that wanted to know who you **really** were, and how you were **really** doing. As she matured as a Christian woman, it became clear that God had His hand of direction on her for whom she was to become. Lallah studied Scripture ferociously, always trying to discover how it related to everyday life. She became intensely interested in the Old Testament and has literally worn out several Bibles. When her elementary teaching career was put on hold to raise our three young boys, Lallah became increasingly knowledgeable of Scripture. Lallah turned to Christian Counseling as a new occupation when our sons were grown and out of the house. She also began speaking for women's retreats, as well as preaching occasionally at local churches. Soon she was doing several large retreats each year for different churches around the Mid-Atlantic region. Marriage counseling continued to grow with referrals from multiple local pastors who would recommend Christian counseling for selected couples in their church. At the same time she pursued ordination with the International Church of the Foursquare Gospel. For the past twenty years she has served as Assistant Pastor at her church in Westminster, MD. Over the years, Lallah has turned to drafting her thoughts, studying Scripture, and committing biblical principles to print. This book is her first attempt at publishing anything that she has formally written. Having observed first hand this transition over the years, I am so impressed with the desire she possesses to complete this task before moving on to whatever God has next for her life. I've been privileged to watch this process unfold, critique it with what limited literary skills I have, and observe the creation of her first work. Praise God for the godly people who have spoken into her life and encouraged her to set foot down this new path. God bless her on this journey.

Walter F. Brilhart

PREFACE

Three years ago a man walked into my counseling office. He was a new client. He was a pastor and I had previous knowledge that he walked in the prophetic. Before we had opportunity to begin the session he looked at me and said, "On the way over here God told me to tell you that you are to write a book." After a few moments of my deer-in-the-headlights response, outwardly I politely said something generic like, "Well, thank you." Inwardly I thought, "Me? Write a book? You must have the wrong gal." Brushing the topic aside, we began the session.

One month later I was speaking at a conference on the other side of the country. Following the session the pastor of the church sought me out and said, "While you were speaking, God told me to tell you that you are to write a book." Again, deer-in-the-headlights. I began to think maybe this is something pastors typically say to people they really didn't know. Actually I know better than that, but I was beginning to get a little unnerved.

Three months later I was having lunch with a dear godly friend and she said, "You know, I'm not sure, but I have this feeling that you are supposed to write a book." Several months after that, the scenario was repeated. This time it was from someone I barely knew at the time, but has since become a dear friend and sister in the Lord.

Alright Lord, a confirmation by two or three. I think I need to pay attention. But in all honesty, I wasn't hearing that from God. I was totally clueless of what I was supposed to be writing. I felt totally inadequate. So I convinced myself that all these messengers were just being nice and complimentary. I tucked the idea away; although every once in a while it would come out and mess with me. Whenever that happened I would feel a tinge of excitement, some guilt that I wasn't doing what God wanted me to do, and a lot of angst over what in the world this book was supposed to be about.

Then God began weaving together three of my passions; His Word, specifically the Old Testament; prayer; and our nation. He would wake me in the middle of the night to "download" a message. He would send me to the computer (with which I did not have an endearing relationship to begin with) and much to my amazement, my fingers would fly.

Day and night He continued to fill my thoughts, to the point that I am sure my dear husband felt very neglected, but was still very supportive. Once he said, "I have never seen you this passionate about anything."

I began to relate to the prophet Jeremiah when he said, "it was like fire in his bones." I would be in the middle of doing something, like cooking or eating dinner, and would have to stop to run to the computer. You will be glad to know that the computer and I now understand one another a little more clearly, and have a slightly better relationship.

This book is the culmination of this whole process. It has been an exciting, thrilling, and awesome ride. I know I have been stretched, have grown, and learned much through the process. I am humbled that God would lay such a message so powerfully on my heart.

Pastor Jack Hayford, who is fondly known throughout the world as Pastor Jack, once said, "A message needs to be informational, inspirational, incarnational, and impartational in order to be transformational. My prayer has been that this book would include all those things. My prayer is that this book stirs you, challenges you, inspires you, empowers you, and drives you to the kind of prayers that have reached the Throne of Grace and have changed history. My prayer is that thousands would join forces across this nation, that we would rise up to be the remnant in our time, and that we would walk in the true calling of the Church. May we, on our watch, be history makers.

TABLE OF CONTENTS

1
UNLEASH YOUR IMAGINATION!
Genesis 1

Let's start at the very beginning...that's a very good place to start. So goes the song of the beloved musical The Sound of Music, as Maria taught the Von Trapp children to sing.

Great idea – but let's be honest, Maria did not really start at the very beginning. For **the** very beginning is found in a beautiful garden named Eden that was filled with the melodious songs of birds. Now *that* is a great place to start.

Beginning...the word itself prompts thoughts of newness. The Garden of Eden was a clean slate upon which God, the Creator of all things, could write His plan within the hearts of Adam and Eve. And so He did, as He walked daily with them in the splendor of this magnificent paradise.

Scripture gives us only glimpses into the times they spent together, and the conversations they shared. We truly don't know how long they shared this sweet communion. It might have been just a day; it might have been hundreds of years. But it's fun to imagine all the possibilities wrapped up in the creation story.

God has given us the incredible gift of imagination. Engaging this gift as we read the Scripture can cause its stories to come to life. Imagination can help us enter into a scene that might otherwise seem distant and irrelevant. Releasing our imagination can help us relate more personally to the principles of the Word. It can enable us to have a deeper and clearer understanding of its many truths.

When we unleash our imagination in this manner, there is a need for caution. What we imagine as we read Scripture is never as important or valid as the written Word of God itself. Although it may help us to explore more deeply, or develop a scenario more fully, it never surpasses Scripture. We always need to discern the difference between our imagination and God's actual Word. If what we imagine does not line up with Scripture, or takes us on a path that challenges the Word, let there be no question as to which has to go. The Word of God endures above all things forever.

Giving our imagination freedom to intersect the Scripture cannot be a hurried process. It is a matter of pondering, questioning, and allowing our senses to experience the stories and scenes. We must be able to slow our world and our minds down, quiet ourselves, and connect with the words we are reading. We must give the Holy Spirit permission, time, and space to ignite our imagination.

For example, envision with me the day God presented Adam with each of the animals to be named. Can you conceive the depth of amazement he must have experienced as he beheld God's creativity expressed in each one? Can you picture him rolling on the ground in laughter as he watched the long-legged and long-necked giraffe figure out how to get a drink of water? Can you picture him scratching his head in confusion as the tortoise played "now you see me, now you don't?" Do you suppose he was amused by the waddle of the duck-billed platypus? Do you think Adam got his first shower when the elephant let loose a trunk full of water in his direction? Can you hear the chuckles from the depth of his belly as mischievous monkeys chased one another from tree to tree? Can you sense the awe that overwhelmed him as he stroked the mane of the majestic lion? Can you imagine the tenderness that flooded his heart as he nuzzled his face in the soft wool of the lamb? Can you picture the sheer delight on the face of God as he watched Adam's amazement at each creature?

That was fun, wasn't it? What a day that must have been! Releasing our imagination can be exciting, amusing, and joyful. It can also be challenging, inspiring, adventuresome, and convicting. Imagination is a wondrous gift given to man and man alone.

God chose to make mankind in His image. Although all creation reflects His glory,[1] we are the only created beings who are assigned to reflect His character. The word "imagination" begins with the word image. By its very definition imagination enables us to be creative. Therefore, the gift of imagination enables us to reflect God's creative character.

When we deny or squelch the expression of our imagination, we essentially limit our ability to reflect God's character. We also hinder our ability to wonder and create. *When we do not give our imaginations permission to impact God's Word, we can hinder the Word's impact on us.* Sadly, at times we allow Holy Spirit inspired passages to remain just black words on a white page; or we allow God-breathed messages to be nothing more than stories from long ago. Lord, forgive us.

Yet when we unleash our imaginations to delve deeply into what is being said; when we envision the scenes and apply our senses to the pages of Scripture, suddenly those very same black and white words explode with life-giving power.

Have you ever pictured the scene when a donkey spoke to Balaam?[2] What must that have looked like? I would love to have been hiding somewhere in the bushes to witness that one. I think it's one of the most hysterical passages in Scripture; the thought of it makes me laugh!

Have you ever listened to the waves clapping (yes, clapping, not lapping) against the shore as Jesus walked by?

Have you ever listened for the belly laugh Jesus might have had to suppress as he watched Zacchaeus climb that tree? (I hope you don't think it irreverent that Jesus would laugh heartily. Maybe that was the beginning of holy laughter.) Have you slowly breathed in the fragrance of the perfume poured out on Jesus' feet as Mary prepared His body for burial? Or have you smelled the stench of those whose bodies were eaten away with leprosy?

Have you ever allowed yourself to connect with the emotions of people in Scripture? Have you ever imagined the intensity and complexity of their various feelings? Can you put yourself in the place of the priests when the Shekinah glory of God descended upon Solomon's temple? Can you imagine the breath-taking awe that fell so heavily upon them that they could not stand or minister? Have you allowed the ecstatic joy of women whose sons were returned to them from death, well up in you? Or have you felt the utter heart wrenching anguish of the women whose baby boys were ripped from their nurturing arms to be run through with a sword before their very eyes?

Have you felt the confusion and fear of the disciples that dark and evil night when Roman soldiers arrested their Master? Have you heard the uncontrollable sobs of the women who stood at the foot of the cross? Can we even begin to imagine the intense emotions the disciples experienced when they beheld the beaten and bloodied body of the One they loved so dearly? Can we imagine their depth of despair and hopelessness as they laid Him in a cold and dark tomb? And then...and then...is it possible to feel their confusion mixed with ecstasy and exhilaration, as He stood upright before them in His glorious resurrected body?

We could go on and on. Actually, I would love to. I will leave that up to you, dear reader, as you turn the pages of your own Bible. I wish we could talk about each and every story; each and every teaching. I pray as you take in the daily bread He has given us that it will not be just a meal, but a magnificent feast, prepared by the Master Chef Himself. Each and every word of Scripture is power-packed and life-inspiring.

So much said; so much unsaid. So much only hinted at. So much I want to know. So many questions I have. So much left open to our imagination.

Imagination is the key to possibilities. Remember, imagination is a gift given by God to man, and man alone. There is an integral connection between this gift of imagination and **what if.** As we allow our imagination to intersect with **what is,** we unlock the door to **what if.** When we walk through that door of **what if,** a whole new realm is opened up to us. When we apply **what if,** we realize things do not need to remain as they are. Scripture says God called things that were not as though they were.[3] The intersection of our imagination and **what if** unleashes the possibilities of what could be. It opens the door from what we see with our physical eyes in the physical realm, to what might be seen with our spiritual eyes in the spiritual realm. **What if** encourages us to move beyond the everyday normal, the status quo, the mundane, the ordinary, and the common. **What if** challenges us to pursue the extraordinary, the remarkable, and the excellent. **What if** stimulates our thinking to consider things beyond our norm. **What if** stirs our faith to believe in and trust for miracles. **What if** inspires us to be history changers and history makers. **What if** emboldens us to contend for the supernatural.

That is the journey on which we are about to embark as we travel through the pages of the Holy Scripture and look at individuals who dared to contend for **what if.** They were just like us, but they dared to believe that their actions and their prayers could turn the tide of history, could impact the future, and could bring about a different and unexpected result.

I believe that is what we desperately need at this hour in history. I believe God is looking for men and women who will courageously and boldly, earnestly and persistently, contend for **what if.** I believe He is looking for those who will not settle for the status quo, who are not satisfied with the ordinary nor the normal, who will not succumb to a standard of living that is beneath what God ordained for those who were created in His image. I believe He is looking for men and women, young and old, who will declare the truth of God among our generation. I believe His eye is searching for those who will proclaim the power and possibilities of the Almighty during this crossroad in history.

If that is the cry of your heart, then I invite you to join me on this journey. Are your bags packed? You won't need much - just your Bible, a hungry heart, and a wide open imagination into which God can pour secret delights.

*Father, thank You for creating us in your image. Thank You for the beauty of this world that You created for our pleasure. Thank You for the gift of imagination. Would You cause that gift to burst forth within each one of us, so that we may perceive with greater clarity the world around us? Especially when we read Your Word, Lord, let our imaginations flow and bring life to what is written. Cause our imaginations to expand our understanding and help us to see the possibilities that are there. Let our imaginations intersect the **what is**, and fill us with the **what if.** In Jesus' Name, Amen.*

PERSONAL REFLECTION

1. Assess your imagination. On a scale of one to ten, (one being the least and ten being the greatest) where would you measure the use of your imagination?

2. What have been the factors in your life that have either encouraged or discouraged the use of your imagination?

3. How would you define the "**what if**" factor?

4. Select a story in the Bible. It can be either in the Old or New Testament. First, read through the passage in its entirety. Then read it several times again, allowing yourself to envision the sights around, smell the odors or fragrances, perhaps feel the wind or water, or whatever may be tactile, and listen for the sounds that might be there. Some stories even allow our taste to come into play, like the changing of water into wine or the feeding of the five thousand. Try to identify with the emotions of the people who are in the story. Imagine their reactions and inner thoughts. Record below what you imagined. Did the story take on deeper meaning for you? Did this help you identify with the characters in the story better? Did you grasp some principles that you may not have before? Do you think this will help you remember the story better?

2
FROM THE CALL TO THE FALL
Genesis 1–3

As we begin our journey, let's go back and find Adam and Eve where we left them in the Garden of Eden. Observing them, we might feet slightly overdressed.

Take a moment to look around the Garden. Drink in its resplendent beauty, vibrant with color. Breathe in the sweet fragrances of exotic flowers. Listen to the joyful yet soothing music of nature. Feel the warmth of the sun as it wraps you in a blanket of perfect temperature and comfort. See its rays of light glisten and dance on the water. Be amazed as you watch the lion and the lamb, the deer and the tiger, and the bear and the kitten romp and play together. Is it not the most magnificent and glorious setting you have ever seen?... Selah.

These things are easy to imagine because most of us have been exposed to all of them to some degree. And even if we have not personally encountered a lion or a bear, National Geographic Magazine and the world of technology have certainly allowed us to experience them vicariously.

But there is something in the Garden that is foreign to us. It is something more difficult for us to imagine. It is something nearly impossible for our finite minds to grasp. It is the absence of sin and the inescapable presence of purity, innocence, safety and all-encompassing peace.

Have you ever lived a day, or even an hour, in this world that was totally – and I mean totally – free from sin? I have not. Whether that sin is within the depths of my own heart, a mess of my own making, the sin of someone close to me, or the sin of mankind in general, I have never experienced an extended period of time when life has not been tainted in some way by the ravages of sin. The closest I can personally identify with the innocence and purity of Eden is in those brief but heavenly moments when I am fully surrendered at the foot of the cross, or when I have gone "beyond the veil" into the Holy of Holies and am wrapped in the glory of God's Presence. I would love to live there. But to be honest, I don't; and I can't. That is a mistake of my own making.

Genesis 2:25 says of Adam and Eve, *"they were naked and unashamed."* It is the last description of them before that fateful day when they yielded to the cunning trickery of the enemy. Unashamed is the only emotion Scripture says they had. We can imagine or presume they felt others, such as joy, love, and peace. But the Word of God simply tells us they were unashamed.

Shamelessness. Pause a moment and ponder that word and all it suggests. No shame - no shame about anything. It is profound. I have never encountered someone who did not have something in their life about which they did not experience shame. Shamelessness means there was **nothing** –absolutely **nothing -** with which they were burdened. There was **no thing** that oppressed them under the unbearable weight of shame. No shame means there was no disobedience, no pride, no jealousy, no fear, no anger, no competition, no malice, no rebellion, no arrogance, no suppression, no lying, no deception, no doubt, no anxiety, no hatred, no hidden motive, no wrong choices, no negativity, no failures, no mistakes – **NO SIN.**

I think you get the picture. We could fill the page with all the things with which we struggle on a daily basis, but were absent from the Garden where Adam and Eve resided. None of those things were there in the slightest measure.

Hard to imagine, isn't it?

What was there in abundance was joy unspeakable, love abounding, peace beyond understanding, patience without boundaries, selflessness of heart, mutual submission, devoted obedience, complete shamelessness, and the Presence of the Almighty. Sounds like a place I would not only like to visit; I would like to live there. How about you?

Forgiveness, mercy, and grace were not even needed. They were being reserved for a future time.

Until that fateful day.

In the midst of all this bliss and goodness of the Garden, God daily walked and talked with Adam and Eve. During this time Jehovah God, Elohim, shared His heart with them. He poured out His love upon them. He shared His vision for things to come. He instructed them in His ways. He invited them to partner with Him in the rule and reign of His magnificent creation. To none of the other creatures did He extend this invitation.

God blessed Adam and Eve and He said to them, *"Be fruitful and increase in number; fill the earth and subdue it. Rule over the fish of the sea and the birds of the air and over every living creature that moves on the ground."*[4]

Did you catch the words *rule and subdue*? The King James Version of the Bible uses the phrase *"have dominion over."* In essence, God was deputizing Adam and Eve to have power and authority over the entirety of His creation on Earth.

One might think, "Seriously God? Seriously? That is a huge responsibility! Have you thought this through? Do you seriously think it's a good idea?" Adam and Eve were still wet behind the ears. The mud from which Adam had been formed was hardly dry yet. The opening in his side from which Eve was fashioned could not possibly have been completely healed! They had no experience, much less a resume that would qualify them for such leadership responsibility. Wouldn't one of the angels have been better suited for such a mammoth undertaking?

Yet God, in His glorious omniscience, chose to promote Adam and Eve to the position. He placed the future of planet Earth in the hands of these two novices. Truth is, they were far more suited than even the highest angels, for the Spirit of God Himself had been breathed into them at their creation. It was that Spirit from which they would rule.

Have you ever known of a man or woman who passed on to their son(s) or daughter(s) something they had devoted their lifetime to build and develop? The transference is typically not something haphazard or impulsive. The process is usually accompanied by much thought, introspection, evaluation, consideration and preparation. On the one hand, it is a time of celebration, as the parent rejoices in anticipation of their children's future success. On the other hand, it can also be a time of painful separation, as they relinquish something into which they have invested so much of their time, talents, energies, finances, and even their identity. That separation might be laced with apprehension. There are no guarantees of how the child(ren) will maintain or continue the legacy. There are no assurances that the heir(s) will value, appreciate, or honor the gift that is given to them. No matter how much instruction, mentoring, or coaching they have been given ahead of time, future success will lay solely in their hands. There are no guarantees that the recipients will fulfill the plans, purposes, or aspirations of their parent.

I wonder if it was like that for God. As he surveyed His creation, perfect in every aspect, I wonder what He must have felt when He placed it in the hands of these two apprentices. Unlike the earthly parent, however, God had complete foreknowledge of what they would do.

But God is sovereign. Despite what we may think through the advantage of hindsight, the decision was fully God's to make. For a period of time all went exceedingly well in the Garden of Eden.

Until that fateful day.

Until that fateful day that literally turned the world upside down and inside out for every living creature; not only for those alive at the time, but for all those who would follow through the ages.

Until that fateful day of wrenching, tearing, and upheaval, when all that was perfect became distorted into something imperfect, unfamiliar, and so undesirable.

Until that fateful day, when those who knew no shame were covered with it from head to toe.

How do we know they went from shamelessness to shame in the blink of an eye? The first thing they did was hide. That's what shame does – it causes us to hide. It causes us to separate. It causes us to cover ourselves, hoping no one will know, no one will notice, and no one will suspect. Shame drives a wedge in our relationship with God and one another. It imprisons us with chains of embarrassment, humiliation, and disgrace.

On that fateful day, shamelessness departed, and shame invaded the heart of man.

On that fateful day, all the angels of God were gathered at the precipice of heaven, witnessing the scene taking place below, where Eve and the serpent were front and center.

Can you picture with me the angels jerking fully to alert as they heard the first word come forth from the serpent as he enticed Eve? The angels of Heaven were eerily familiar with this voice. It was the voice of the one who had once enjoyed the magnificence of Heaven with them.[5] It was the voice of the one who had rebelled when he tried to exalt himself above their

Master. It was the voice of the one who had cunningly incited a third of the angels to side with him in the rebellion against the Almighty.[6] Oh yes, they knew this voice all too well. They knew of what he was capable. Can you see them positioning themselves, poised to intervene and protect God's prized creation the instant He gave the command? Waiting... waiting...waiting...surely He would send them forth! Surely they could dispel this evil one with one lethal blow!

Can you hear the resounding "Noooooooooooooo!!!!!!!!!!!" that reverberated throughout the heavenly realm as Eve took hold of the fruit, raised it to her lips, and sunk her teeth into its pulp? Can you hear the horrendous thud that shook them to their core at the falling of Adam and Eve from their position of dominion to their new place of slavery? Can you hear the clanking of invisible chains of bondage being wrapped around them? Can you detect their exhaling breath as the Spirit of the Living God exited their being?

In an instant everything...*everything*...changed.

It is easy for us to play "Monday morning quarterback" as we view the scene from afar. If we could rewrite this pivotal portion of Scripture, I wonder what it might look like. If only we had been consulted during the original planning we might have offered a number of plausible options. If we had been consulted we might have suggested to God that turning the control over to Adam and Eve might not be such a good idea. We might have presented the Creator with a list of alternatives, a list of substitute possibilities, or a list of **what ifs.** Maybe there could be a do-over.

What if God never created the serpent? **What if** He had totally eliminated Satan when he rebelled in Heaven? **What if** God had orchestrated the scenario so that the serpent never had access to those created in His image? Surely he could have done that.

What if God had prevented evil from entering the serpent, or any other creature, in the first place? Surely God could have done that.

Yes, surely he could have. But if He had, Adam and Eve would have never been presented with a *choice.* They would have never known free will. They would have been mere puppets. Their love, devotion, obedience, and worship would have never been tested. *Love that is void of the option to choose, is not love at all.* It is merely a programmed response. God desired those created in His image to love Him because they wanted to, not because they had to. Jesus told his disciples the night He was betrayed, *"If you love me, you will obey what I command."* [7] Obedience speaks love to God. It is one of the primary languages through which He receives love from us. The ultimate lover of our souls desires that we express our love for Him through obedience to His commands and a desire for Him above all else.

What if God had given the command for the angels to swoop down and rescue Eve, the damsel in distress? **What if** they had been given the go ahead to crush the serpent, rendering him and his insidious scheme powerless? **What if** the angelic army of God had been given permission to evict Satan from the Garden?

Surely God could have sent forth that command, and that day would have been saved. But again, doing so would have eliminated the free will God had gifted to Adam and Eve. Had the angels rescued them that day, they would already have abdicated their right to rule and have dominion.

What if Adam had been by Eve's side to step in and be her superhero? Where was he, anyway? We often, perhaps jokingly, assume that Adam had wandered off somewhere. We often conclude he was not where he was supposed to be and not fulfilling his role as her protector. **What if** Adam was not the one who had wandered off? **What if** it were Eve? **What if** she had been lured away by the cunning tactics of the serpent? **What if** she was not where she was supposed to be? Have you ever noticed how much more susceptible we are to temptation when we are by ourselves, or in the wrong places? Have you ever noticed that the enemy has a way of isolating us while he makes sin so enticing and appealing?

What if Adam and Eve had been together when the serpent addressed Eve? Would they have been a united force that could have resisted the temptation? Perhaps. Would they have reminded one another of God's goodness and instruction? Perhaps.

But then the concept of personal choice and personal responsibility with God would not have been presented. None of us can have a relationship with God through someone else. No one can make the decision to serve and obey God for someone else. We all know there are many times we would like to. How many spouses yearn to make the choice for their husband or wife? How many parents grieve when they see their children walking a path contrary to God's ways? How many parents want, and even try, to redirect the path their adult children have chosen?

Yet from the beginning, God has determined that following Him must be a personal decision. The closeness of one's walk with Him is a personal decision. Adam could not make it for Eve, and Eve could not make it for Adam. God would not honor or permit that. Eve had to make it for herself. Adam had to make it for himself. You and I have to make it for ourselves. Our spouse, our children, and our loved ones have to make it for themselves. We can coerce and manipulate all we want, but it is to no avail.

Perhaps it was not a coincidence that Adam and Eve were not together at this particular moment. Perhaps God had arranged it that way so that they were each confronted with the choice on their own. Perhaps this was a crossroads they had to face alone.

What if the serpent had gone to Adam before Eve? Surely Adam would have resisted...wouldn't he?

Maybe. We will never know for sure, at least not on this side of eternity. But if so, then Adam would not have been presented with the dilemma of whom he desired to please the most – his God, or his beautiful bride. He would not have been confronted with the choice of whom he would listen to, and by whom he would be led – His Maker, or the one He had made? He would not have had to choose whom he would trust – his Creator, or the created.

What if they had remembered that God had forbidden them to eat of the fruit of the tree of knowledge?

They did. Eve even reminded the serpent of that significant fact. Somewhere in the conversation, that fact became distorted and lost its significance.

Consider something with me for a moment. This is a place we might give wings to our imagination. Was there a reason Eve would have realized this voice speaking to her was dangerous? Up to this point she had never encountered danger or evil. Up to this point danger was not a possibility or reality to her. Perhaps in Eve's thinking evil was not on her radar screen.

Up to this point all she had known was good, for everything in the Garden had been created by God and everything God created was good. God had created the serpent. Perhaps in Eve's thinking the serpent was therefore good.

Perhaps she had engaged in conversations with the serpent in the past. I imagine Adam and Eve were able to converse with all the animals.

Scripture tells us two things about the serpent: he was a wise and cunning creature, and he was relegated to crawl on his belly after the Fall. Being wise and cunning, perhaps at one time the serpent was a good and interesting communicator. Perhaps Eve and the serpent were accustomed to sharing enjoyable conversations. Perhaps Eve was in the habit of discussing life in the Garden with the serpent. Perhaps at one time the serpent stood upright and was a magnificent creature. If he did stand upright, and most of the other creatures did not, perhaps Eve saw the serpent as being more comparable to Adam and Eve.

This is all speculation of course, but it is possible. If so, then perhaps Eve had no reason to question the serpent's motives. Perhaps her defense mechanisms were down; or more accurately, perhaps they weren't there at all because she didn't know she needed them. Perhaps she couldn't fathom anyone doing something contrary to God's command.

The enemy saw her vulnerability. He saw her innocence and took full advantage. He entered one that had access to her trust. He used the vessel of the serpent as his mouthpiece to deceive, to deliver his sinister plan, and to strike a deadly blow.

Eve was totally caught off guard; she was blindsided. Perhaps she didn't discern that the spirit of God's arch enemy had inhabited the serpent. Perhaps she didn't realize the voice was the voice of evil.

Isn't that how the enemy works in all our lives? He watches for our vulnerabilities, then he ever so slyly slips his deception into our hearts and minds. Sometimes he uses things or people with which we are familiar, and he confuses us with his crafty trickery. He makes his temptations seem logical, harmless, or innocuous. He slowly and cunningly leads us astray, while all the time poisoning us with deceptive and empty promises. Often we are not even aware until it's too late. So it was with Eve on that fateful day.

What if – just **what if** Adam and Eve had remembered the mandate? **What if** the words *rule and reign* had rung loudly in their ears? **What if** Eve had trusted in her God given authority over all creatures? **What if** she had remembered that the serpent was merely a created creature over which she had been instructed to rule? **What if** she remembered she, not the serpent, had been created in God's image? **What if** she had not engaged in conversation with him, but had remembered she was called to tell the serpent what to do, and not the other way around? **What if** she had stood in the position of authority that was rightfully hers? **What if** she had acted in that authority? **What if** she had used her authority to silence this one who dared to question her God? **What if** Adam and Eve had embraced their God-given identity as an extension of Him on planet Earth? **What if** they had walked in that identity as His authoritative representatives?

What if? Then Adam and Eve would have walked in victory; at least for that moment. But somewhere along the line there would have been a fateful succumbing to the temptation of the enemy. There had to be. The gift of choice and free will opened the door for that. But that gift opened the door to another gift – the most incredible gift – the gift of a Savior. Before God began creation He knew sin would enter the picture someday. He already had in place a plan to reverse the mess we would make.

That plan had a Name – it was Immanuel, God with us, Jesus. In the fullness of time He would be sent to be like us and dwell among us. In the fullness of time God Himself would clothe Himself in our flesh. He would be nailed to a cross on a hill named Calvary where the full measure of our punishment would be unleashed upon Him. As His bloodied, beaten, distorted-beyond-recognition body would hang on that cross, every act of disobedience from that fateful day in the Garden to the end of times would be laid entirely upon Him. He would bear the stripes for our healing. He would take the shame for our transgressions. He would pay the price – in full. Forgiveness would flow in a stream of red that soaked into the dirt from which Adam was formed. And the greatest expression of amazing love and amazing grace ever imagined would be forever extended to all mankind.

Jesus died upon that cross. But God's plan of redemption was not finished at the cross. For after three days, His bloodless body rose from the dead. His resurrected body remained on earth for forty more days, during which He continued to teach His disciples. Then He ascended to Heaven where He lives forevermore. And then He sent the Holy Spirit to live within His followers.

The Spirit of God had departed from Adam and Eve that fateful day in the Garden when they obeyed the words of Satan over the Word of their God. Since that day the Spirit of God dwelt *with* man, but had never lived *within* man. Since that day man could witness the power of God, but the power of God did not inhabit man. Since that day, man lost the power and authority given to him through God's mandate.

When the Holy Spirit was poured out following Christ's ascension, it was a new day. It was not a fateful day; it was a marvelous day.

On that marvelous day, the Holy Spirit of God came to live *within* man.

On that marvelous day, the Holy Spirit of God was sent to indwell man.

On that marvelous day, the power and authority lost in the Garden was restored to man.

That day was a day of reversal, not just for those alive at that time, but for all who would follow throughout the ages. **What if** we live our lives as though the Holy Spirit lives within us? **What if** we remember and rehearse the mandate given us? **What if** we recognize the power and authority that is available to us? **What if** we realize that greater is He Who is in us than he who is in the world?[8] **What if** we use that authority to push back the gates of Hell?[9] **What if** we operate in that authority to bring the Kingdom of God to Earth?

It was not God's plan that the angels, mighty and majestic as they were, would rescue Adam and Eve that day. It was His original plan that the rescue and deliverance be carried out one day in the future by the second Adam – Jesus the Christ.[10] His plan of redemption included not only the forgiveness of our sins, but the shattering of our bondages, and empowerment through the Holy Spirit.

From the beginning, God had a superior plan, and an eternal plan. The sin of Adam and Eve could not and did not nullify it. Even though God had told them they would die on the day they ate of the tree of knowledge, the story was not over. Thank God; the story was not over.

Father, thank You for Your plan of salvation. Thank You for not giving up on mankind. Thank You for not abandoning us. Thank You for sending Jesus. Thank You for the forgiveness that came through His work on the cross. Thank You that He rose from the dead and conquered death. Thank You for sending the Holy Spirit. Thank You for being the restorer of all things. Thank You for the hope we have in You. In Jesus' Name, Amen.

PERSONAL REFLECTION

1. Do you have any new or fresh insights regarding the Creation story?

2. Think back through your life. How did you deal with issues that caused you shame? How did shame make you feel? What did it cause you to do?

3. Do you have an assurance in your heart that you have received Christ as your personal Savior?

If not, you can have that assurance now. Acknowledge that God is sovereign. Take some time to thank Him for His plan of salvation. Confess your sins to Jesus and receive His forgiveness. Surrender your life to Him and give Him permission to take control. Invite Jesus into your heart, spirit, and life to be your Savior and Lord.

If you have prayed that prayer for the first time, congratulations! You have just made the most important decision of your life! It is vital for you to grow in your walk with the Lord. Just as a newborn baby needs to be fed, so our newly born spirits need to be fed. God has given us His Word as that food. Get a translation of the Bible that is easy for you to understand. Feed on His food everyday so that it nourishes your spirit and soul. Prayer, worship, and fellowship with other believers are also essential aspects of our growth. I am praying even now that you will find a group of believers with whom you can grow in your new life.

Welcome to the family of God my new brother or sister!

4. What is your understanding of the power and authority we have been given through the indwelling presence of the Holy Spirit?

5. What three **what ifs** speak to you the most? Would you add any?

3

ABRAHAM – FRIEND OF GOD
Genesis 17-18

No, the story was not over; far from it. We may think it should have been. We are quick to rush to judgement and condemn. But praise God; the decision did not lay in our hands. It rested solely in the hands of the Almighty Who sits on a throne of grace and mercy.

In reality the story was just beginning. So let us move forward, turning the pages of Scripture as they reveal to us God's plan of redemption for the horrible hot mess that had been made.

After reading through the many "begats" (what I refer to as the "hard name, skip its"), we are introduced to a man named Abram. The story of Abram begins in Genesis 12, just nine chapters after the fall of Adam and Eve.

If we compare these twelve chapters to the length of the entire Bible, we might come to the conclusion that they covered a relatively short span of time. We would be wrong. Actually those twelve chapters comprise a period of two thousand years, give or take a few. Adding together the life spans of those born between Adam and Abram there were approximately two thousand years; between the birth of Abram and Christ there were two thousand years; and between the birth of Christ and present day there are approximately two thousand years. So this small sliver of the Bible between Genesis 1 and Genesis 12 comprises one-third of man's existence on planet Earth.

Scripture does not divulge much of God's interaction with His creation during this first two thousand year period. We do know that people carried out the mandate to be fruitful and multiply, but they could not walk in righteous power, authority, and dominion the way God intended them. Whatever power and authority they wielded had become increasingly distorted by sin. Each generation dove to new depths of depravity and perversion.

In the midst of this darkness were some rays of light. Throughout history, even in the most heinous of times, there seems to be a remnant of people who chose good over evil; who hold onto hope of a better way; and who choose to believe in a greater power than themselves or this world.

There were a few of them between Adam and Abram. Enoch was one. The Scripture says Enoch walked with God and he was no more.[11] Apparently, God was so pleased with His fellowship with Enoch, that He just took him to glory. Noah was one. God saved Noah and his family from the flood that destroyed everyone else. One might say that after Noah, mankind got a "do-over," a second chance to get it right. Although the opportunity may have been presented, sadly we did not take advantage of it. Noah's own son allowed sin to enter his heart and the downward spiral of sin began again.

Nine generations after Noah stepped out of the ark, Abram was born.[12] Until this time God had spoken individually to certain people, but he was beginning something new with the call of Abram. Through Abram, God was creating a nation of people that would be His own.

So in Genesis 12:1 God instructed Abram, who was seventy-five years old at the time, to leave the place of his birth and travel to a land called Canaan. Later that land came to be known as the Promised Land; today we know it as Israel. Accompanied by his nephew Lot, and his wife Sarai, Abram packed all his worldly possessions and set out on the journey. Having no map, no AAA to call, no GPS, no Siri, and no internet, Abram was obedient to God's call and was led by the Spirit to this new, strange, and foreign land.

Throughout his journey God was faithful to meet with Abram, to assure him, to make promises to him, to provide for him, to protect him, and to intervene on his behalf. God even "cut covenant" with Abram.

Genesis 15 and 17 are what I refer to as hallmark chapters in the Bible. I believe every Jew and Christian should be familiar with them. They contain the roots of our Jewish and Christian heritage. They describe the manner in which this blood covenant was cut and give the promises God spoke forth.

So the LORD said to him, "Bring me a heifer, a goat and a ram, each three years old, along with a dove and a young pigeon."

Abram brought all these to him, cut them in two and arranged the halves opposite each other; the birds, however, he did not cut in half. Then birds of prey came down on the carcasses, but Abram drove them away.

As the sun was setting, Abram fell into a deep sleep, and a thick and dreadful darkness came over him. Then the LORD said to him, "Know for certain that your descendants will be strangers in a country not their own, and they will be enslaved and mistreated four hundred years. But I will punish the nation they serve as slaves, and afterward they will come out with great possessions. You, however, will go to your fathers in peace and be buried at a good old age. In the fourth generation your descendants will come back here, for the sin of the Amorites has not yet reached its full measure."

When the sun had set and darkness had fallen, a smoking firepot with a blazing torch appeared and passed between the pieces. On that day the LORD made covenant with Abram and said, "To your descendants I give this land, from the river of Egypt to the great river, the Euphrates – the land of the Kenites, Kenizzites, Kadmonites, Hittites, Perizzites, Rephaites, Amorites, Canaanites, Girgashites and Jebusites."[13]

God's request that Abram cut a heifer, a goat, and a ram in two seems bizarre and barbaric to us living in the twenty-first century. Abram, on the other hand, understood completely what God was intending. This was the typical procedure used between two parties as they entered into a covenant. This process was similar to our signing contracts today. Normally, both parties would walk between the bloody halves of the carcasses as they stated the terms of the covenant. Their actions were declaring that if either party broke the terms of the covenant, their fate would be like that of the dead animals. Blood covenants were extremely binding.[14]

Abram was expecting God to show up so they could walk through the carcasses together. God, however, did not make an appearance until it was dark and Abram was in a deep slumber. Then, in the form of a smoking firepot and a blazing torch, He passed through the animal halves without Abram. The firepot and the torch were a foreshadowing of how God would one day accomplish the promise He just made to Abram concerning his descendants being led out of slavery. The fact that God waited until Abram was in a deep sleep before He passed through the spilt blood was an incredibly prophetic statement. Essentially, God was saying, "Abram you and your descendants shoulder none of the responsibility in this covenant. I (God) alone shoulder the responsibility. You and your descendants will not incur punishment if the covenant is broken. I (God) will accept all the punishment."

Abram and his descendants did not fulfill their terms of the covenant. Two thousand years after the cutting of this blood covenant, Jesus Christ, the second person of the Godhead, incurred the punishment on the cross, as His body was pierced and His holy blood poured out on the ground.

In Genesis 17 God expounded on the promises and terms of the covenant. After Abram had lived in the new land for twenty-four years, and was the ripe young age of ninety-nine, God spoke some rather specific and amazing things to him. God told Abram that he would be the father of many nations; that some of his descendants would be mighty and powerful kings; that his offspring would be more plentiful than the stars in the sky; that this would be an everlasting covenant not only with Abram but with his descendants; and that the entire land of Canaan would be an everlasting possession for his people.

Who would not be ecstatic over such extraordinary prospects? But there was one small problem. Actually to us it would seem more like an insurmountable problem. All of the promises hinged on Abram having children. Abram was ninety-nine years old. His wife Sarai was almost ninety and way past the age of child bearing. They had never been able to conceive, although they probably tried many times when in their prime. How could they have descendants as numerous as the stars if they had no children? Big problem for us; no problem for God.

It was at this same encounter that God gave the sign of the covenant to Abram and his descendants. All males were to bear in their body the sign of circumcision. It would be a daily and personal reminder of their unique relationship with God and His life giving-promises.

With the giving of this sign, God also changed Abram's name from Abram to Abraham. There is something deeply significant in this name change. The birth name, Abram, meant exalted, noble, or high father. One cannot go through a day, much less a lifetime, without hearing their name over and over. As Abram aged and no children were born from his loins, I wonder if his name became a source of mockery to him. I wonder if every time he heard his name he was reminded of his inability to procreate. I wonder if his name screamed at him, "Failure!" - chiding that he couldn't live up to it. I wonder if hearing his name made the pain of childlessness both more real and less bearable to him.

But oh, how God's grace, compassion, and mercy are revealed in the giving of this new name, Abraham. Abraham means father of multitudes. God's purpose for Abraham was never that he would be an exalted or noble father in and of himself to one or two or even twenty offspring. God's purpose for Abraham was that after he bore the sign of the covenant in his flesh, Abraham would become a father of multitudes that would follow, worship, exalt, and glorify God as Father.

At this time, God proclaimed that Sarai's name would be changed to Sarah. Sarai meant princely. It was a name that definitely spoke of royalty, but was void of any semblance of femininity. In that period of history, a woman's calling and purpose was to bear children. That was the source of her identity, significance, value, and satisfaction. Perhaps each time Sarai heard her name she was cruelly reminded that she was unable to do what seemed easy and normal to most women. Perhaps the very mention of her name screamed the fact that she could not conceive. Perhaps it initiated an internal torment that said she would never nurse a baby at her breast, would never sing a lullaby to hush a little one, or would never know the joy of rocking one of her own flesh and blood to sleep. Perhaps the sound of her own name reinforced that she was anything but feminine.

But the name Sarah means Queen or Mother of Princes. God's plan and purpose for Sarah was never that she be royal in herself, but that her royalty come from being in a covenant relationship with the Almighty. His plan was that the bloodline of royalty come through her, as her descendants would be kings and princes. His plan was that one day in the far future, the King of Kings would make His entrance into this world through the royal lineage that began with Sarah.

That was why God had not allowed Sarai to conceive before this encounter. The child of promise that God planned to come from the union of Abraham and Sarah had to be conceived after Abraham was circumcised. Isaac was the first one born following Abraham's circumcision and therefore was in covenant relationship with God at the time of his conception.

How could Abraham contain himself with all this astounding news? And how was he going to explain this to Sarai? Don't you know that for at least seven decades the longing of Sarai's heart had been for a child? Can't you imagine the disappointment she experienced every month when she realized there was no life in her womb? Could the number of tears that spilled on her pillow each night be counted? She had even devised a way by which Abram could bear a child through her handmaiden, Hagar. That hadn't worked out so well. And that child, Ishmael, had been born before the covenant.

Can you imagine the depth of pain as time and time again Sarai's hopes and dreams were so dashed that she eventually didn't allow herself to hope or dream again? How could Abraham even attempt to stir that longing in her at this stage of their lives? Don't you know he must have been both eager and excited, yet hesitant and dubious to inform his lifelong bride of this news?

Once again the compassion of God intersected their lives. Abraham did not have to have the discussion with Sarah. God himself informed Sarah that her aged body would soon carry and give birth to a son.

And so He, along with two companions, made a house call; or to be more accurate, a tent call. They enjoyed a meal at the couple's home before God dropped the bombshell within ear shot of Sarah that a baby would soon be on the way.

We can completely understand her reaction of unbelief. We can even understand Sarah's covering up her reaction when God called her out on it. Haven't we all done the same at some time or another? Haven't we all at some time given into fear and denied, justified, or rationalized our sin when our hands have been caught in the cookie jar?

Sarah might have been either stinging from the reprimand or stunned speechless, but don't you know that a hundred questions were exploding inside her? God had not come for discussion or debate. He had come to state what was to be. When that was accomplished, the mission, the visit, and the conversation were over. It might have been the original "I hate to eat and run" scenario!

Leaving Sarah to not only clean up after the meal, but to digest this life-changing piece of information, the three visitors got up to leave. Abraham could have stayed to help Sarah sort through the dishes and the news. He could have waved them on their way and then danced with Sarah as they celebrated together something they had desperately desired for what must have seemed like an eternity.

He did not. Although it appeared the visitors had completed their business, Abraham *"walked along with them to see them on their way."*[15] Perhaps Abraham was simply being hospitable. But this small act of accompanying the three travelers put Abraham in an interesting position.

Abraham was about to experience a *"kairos"* moment. In the Greek, there are two words for time. The first is *kronos,* which refers to specific measurements of time, such as a minute, an hour, a week, a month, or a year. The second is *kairos,* which refers to quality of time, or a special time. *Kairos* moments are moments in one's life that are full of opportunity and promise. They are moments that are pregnant with life-transforming potential. They are moments that challenge us and stretch us. How we respond to those *kairos* moments might well determine the destiny of our lives.

If Abraham had chosen to not *"walk along with them and see them on their way,"* he would have completely missed this *kairos* moment. If he had chosen to just see them part of the way and wave good-bye, he would have missed it. But because he chose to walk with them and stay close to them, he was invited to not only experience their presence, but to be privy to their thoughts.

As they walked, God began a conversation. It might have been with His two companions, or it might have been with Himself as He thought out loud. He posed the question, *"Shall I hide from Abraham what I am about to do?"*[16] He continued on, as if processing the thought, *"For Abraham will surely become a great and powerful nation, and all nations on earth will be blessed through him. For I have chosen him, so that he will direct his children and his household after him to keep the way of the LORD by doing what is right and just, so that the LORD will bring about for Abraham what he had promised him."*[17]

This question did not infer that God couldn't figure out the answer, or that He needed someone else's input. It wasn't that God did not already know the answer to the question before He spoke it, for God has all foreknowledge.

The question was not directed *at* Abraham, but it was spoken *for the sake* of Abraham. It was an invitation to Abraham to hear the heart of God as God shared His plans with him. God posed the question to pull Abraham in. God was making a way for Abraham to step into his appointed role as a blesser of the nations. God was wanting Abraham not to just walk with Him, not to just hear the plans, but to partner with Him in what would happen in the lives of the people around him.

Think about it. One of the provisions of the covenant was that Abraham and his descendants would be conduits of God's blessings to the nations of the world. This was both an opportunity and a test for Abraham. Would he step up to the plate and embrace that opportunity so that he was not a bystander, but an active participant in the plans and purposes of the Almighty?

It has been said that the opportunity of a lifetime must be seized during the lifetime of the opportunity. Abraham stepped up to the plate.

God changed the focus of His conversation to the deplorable morality and sin in the cities of Sodom and Gomorrah. He indicated impending judgement was on the way. The other two companions turned away and continued on their journey, but Abraham did not follow them. Instead, he drew closer to God. He turned to face Him. He was about to enter his *kairos* moment. His heart was pounding with concern for the people of Sodom and Gomorrah. He was moved with compassion not just for those he knew there, but for all the people. He was aghast at the thought of their destruction. This was the heart in Abraham for which God was looking.

I imagine this might have been the first time Abraham was exposed to the judgement side of God. But he also knew the merciful and righteous character of God. It was to that side he made his appeal. He was compelled to intervene on behalf of those he had never even met. Abraham made supplication for the city on behalf of the righteous living there. "God, surely You would not bring destruction where there is righteousness, would You?" Abraham began pleading on behalf of the fifty righteous. He met no resistance from God. He was emboldened, and presented his request on behalf of forty-five righteous. He met no resistance from God. He pleaded on behalf of forty, then thirty, then twenty, and finally ten. Once again God acquiesced and Abraham met no resistance.

Now in covenant relationship with the Almighty, Abraham took on the mantel of the intercessor. He appealed to God on behalf of others. His heart was burdened for the welfare and deliverance of their souls. He stepped into his calling as a blesser of nations. At no time did God put forth the least bit of resistance or denial to his supplications.

At no time in his life was Abraham more like the Promised One who would be birthed through his lineage, Christ the Messiah. For Christ Jesus sits at the right hand of the Father, making intercession for each one of us. Abraham seized this opportunity of a lifetime and passed the test.

As the story continued God did not find ten righteous in the city of Sodom and Gomorrah. There were only four. **What if** Abraham had asked God to stay His judgement if there were just four righteous? Truth is, we will never know. The Scripture seems to indicate that God ended the conversation as He turned away. Having compassion on His friend Abraham, God did rescue his family members before destroying the cities with fire and brimstone. Perhaps the point of the conversation was never to withhold judgement from the city, but to engage Abraham and extend the invitation for him to walk in his calling.

There were options along the way that Abraham could have chosen. **What if** Abraham had stayed to help Sarah with the clean-up and had never *"walked with them to see them on their way?"*

Then we would have never had the opportunity to hear the heart and plans of God. He would have never received the invitation to partner with God. The conversation would have never happened. Abraham would not have embraced his *kairos* moment.

How many *kairos* moments have I missed because I was busy doing something else and not walking closely with my Jesus? How many *kairos* moments have you missed? If we want to grow in our relationship with Him and in our callings, time with Him is essential. We must learn to discern what is and what is not needful in our lives. We must learn to set aside things that may seem good, but are not the best. We must realize that what is permissible for others may not be permissible for us if God is calling us to something different. When we are intentional in setting aside time to be with the Lord, we will not be disappointed. He is faithful to meet us. When our desire is to seek His face and know His ways, we will not be confused in our thinking about Him. We will know His character and can act and pray out of the absolute assurance that He is who He says He is, and He will do what He says He will do. God's Word says He shares His secrets with those who love Him. I want to know Him, His character, His ways, His promises, and His secrets. Don't you, too? I know you do.

What if we made it a priority to draw ever closer to the Lord? **What if** we purposed in our hearts to hear His heart? **What if** we were constantly hungry for a "Now" word from heaven? How different would our lives be? How different would our families be? How different would our world be?

What if Abraham had walked off with the two companions as they continued on their journey instead of drawing closer to God? Then he would have known the problem but not sought the Problem Solver.

How many times do we allow our attention to be drawn to an individual instead of to God? How many times do we seek the counsel of others before we go before His Throne of Grace? How many times do we find a pastor or a Bible study teacher that we really admire, and we focus on them more than we do God Himself? We may find ourselves buying every book they write or attending every conference they hold. They may speak truth, they may be gifted by the Holy Spirit, and they may even be anointed in their calling. But if we hang on their every word more than His Word, there is a problem. If we find ourselves talking about them more than we do the One who called them, there is a problem. If we find ourselves more enthralled with their books than we do His Book, there is a problem.

The body of Christ has been blessed with tremendously talented worship leaders and song writers. But do we ever fall into the hazard of following one of these gifted people more than we do the Lord? Do we ever adore worship more than the One Who is to be worshipped? Are we ever so caught up in the musicality of the songs that we miss the message? Are we more enthralled with the anointing of the music than the One who anoints it? Have we gotten to the place where we think we can't really worship unless we have a certain genre of music? Does the music engage our body and soul more than it does our spirit? God is a jealous God. He is fervently jealous for our affection. He will not share His throne with anyone or anything. We need to guard our hearts diligently that they are not captivated by anything other than God, even if those things are godly.

What if we truly sought God above all things and all others? **What if** we truly loved Him with all our heart, all our mind, all our soul, and all our being? Do you suppose we would gain greater access to His throne, greater favor from His heart, and greater answers from His hand than we have ever experienced before? Do you suppose we would approach the Almighty in humble boldness as Abraham did? Do you suppose we would have greater impact to influence the future for good? Do you suppose we would be positioned to bring blessings to the nations? I, for one, would like to try.

What if Abraham had responded in a different manner than he did? **What if** he had been indifferent to the plight of the people living in Sodom and Gomorrah? Or worse yet, **what if** he agreed they deserved punishment? Then he would have missed his *kairos* moment and would not have stepped into God's purpose for his life.

I cannot speak for you, but again, this is a test I have failed too many times. How often have I learned from the news or another source about the hardships of others, and I respond with a nonchalant attitude? How often have I lacked compassion for those I do not know personally? How often have I rushed to judgement concerning the actions of others when I don't know their situations? How often have I condemned them in my heart? More times than I care to admit.

What if all of us would respond to the needs of others – whether we know them or not; whether they are the same skin color as we or not; whether they speak the same language we do or not; whether they have the same life style we do or not –

with compassion, caring, mercy, and intercession? **What if** we put aside the judgements, criticisms, divisions, negativity, and condemnations? **What if** instead, we offered genuine and authentic benevolence for those in need? **What if** our hearts resembled the heart of Abraham, who interceded on the behalf of Sodom and Gomorrah? **What if** our hearts reflected the heart of Jesus, Who is forever forgiving and sits on the seat of mercy? **What if?** The world would certainly be a more pleasant place to live.

    What if Abraham had compassion but it had never manifested in intercession? **What if** he had never pleaded on behalf of the cities because of the righteous? **What if** he had not had the humble boldness to approach God and make supplication? We will never know for sure, but possibly not even Lot and his daughters would have been rescued. Abraham would never have experienced the power of intercession and the incredible willingness of his merciful God.

    What if those who are in covenant relationship with God would draw near to the Almighty and cry out for our nation? There is not a sin committed by Sodom and Gomorrah that is not rampant in America today. Sometimes we think the sin of these two cities was sexual immorality. The prophet Ezekiel tells us that the sin of Sodom and Gomorrah was pride, fullness, idleness, indifference to the poor, various abominations, oppression and brutalization.[18] These and many more atrocities are abundant in our nation. America is positioning herself for judgement.

    What if we would stand upon the precedent set by Abraham and say, "Lord, You who are righteous and full of mercy, would You sweep away the righteous because of the wicked? Far be it from You to do such a thing. Will not You, the Judge of all the earth do right? Lord, if there are fifty thousand that bear Your Name, and are therefore righteous, would you withhold Your judgement? Lord, if there are five thousand in covenant relationship with You, and therefore righteous, will You spare this nation? Lord, it there are five hundred who have accepted the work of Jesus on the cross, and are therefore righteous, will You withhold destruction? Lord, if there are fifty who believe Your Word and trust in You, will You stay Your hand of chastisement? Lord, if there are only five who adhere to You and walk in Your ways, will you forgive and cover our nation with Your mercy?

What if?

Gracious Heavenly Father, we do come to You on behalf of our nation. We know we do not deserve Your forgiveness, grace, or mercy. But we cry out to You to withhold what we do deserve, and send forth what we do not. Lord, may our hearts be sensitive to the conviction of Your Holy Spirit. Burden our hearts with the needs of others. Cause us to lift them before Your throne of grace for their salvation. Remind us of the power of intercession. Impress upon us the need to be persevering in prayer. Astound us with Your answers. Stir within us the purposes and callings You have for each one of us. Open our eyes to the kairos moments you send into our lives. Cause us to step into them and embrace them. Thank you for allowing us to partner with You as You work in our lives, our nation, and our world. In Jesus' Name, Amen.

PERSONAL REFLECTION

1. Have you ever experienced a time you would identify as a *kairos* moment in your life? How did you handle it?

2. What are your thoughts regarding our tendency to follow others more than we follow Jesus? Can you personally identify with it? What are some warning signs and what are some ways we can safeguard our hearts from falling into that trap?

3. Pick a nation in the world that is in turmoil. Research and ask God to show you the needs of the people. Commit to pray for that nation and those people every day for one month. Write below some of the areas you will target in prayer.

4. If you are not already, please begin to pray for our nation on a daily basis. Use current events to generate prayer concerns. Write below any insights God lays on your heart.

5. What three **what ifs** spoke to you the most? Would you add any?

4
THERE'S NO SUCH THING AS A HOLY COW
Exodus 32

Several months after the Lord's visit, Sarah conceived and within the year their one and only son, Isaac, was born, just as God had said.

At his birth Sarah once again laughed. The laughter was different this time. It was not laughter laced with unbelief and mockery. It was laughter birthed in deepest joy and thanksgiving.

Isaac was the son of promise, the first born of the covenant, the first in a very long and everlasting lineage. Isaac had children, and those children had children, and they had children.

The descendants of Abraham had lived in the land for over one hundred years when famine struck and they were desperate for food. This desperation eventually resulted in the great grandchildren of Abraham leaving the land God had promised them and taking up residency in Egypt.

I wonder if they ever realized this transplant would last four hundred twenty years. When they first arrived in Egypt, there was a total of seventy descendants. They were welcomed with opened arms, even esteemed, and given a spacious and fertile place to live.

But several generations later, these seventy had multiplied into the hundreds of thousands. They were no longer embraced with hospitality. The very magnitude of their numbers became a threat to the Egyptians, who began to fear the Hebrews, as the sons of Abraham came to be known. The Egyptians feared the Hebrews would unite, revolt, and take over the land of Egypt. The Egyptians had forgotten what an asset the Hebrews had originally been to them and could only see the potential threat they might be.

The Egyptians' solution was to strip the Hebrews of their freedom and enslave them. What once had been a place of refuge became a place of bondage, hard labor, cruel treatment, and abusive atrocities.

The Hebrews began to cry out to the God of their father Abraham for deliverance. And as He always does, God heard their cry. God raised up a deliverer.

From Moses' birth God had his hand upon him. From his birth, God had a plan and purpose for Moses. As He does for all of us, God orchestrated the events in Moses' life to prepare Moses for his calling.

Moses was probably unaware of the orchestration behind all the twists and turns his life took. We too, are usually oblivious to what God is doing in our lives at the time.

The first third of Moses' life was spent in the palace of Pharaoh. This was highly abnormal because Moses was a Hebrew. At this juncture of history Egyptians abhorred Hebrews, considering them filthy and detestable. God arranged that Moses' true identity remain anonymous. It was in the palace of Pharaoh that Moses learned the skills of leadership he would need later in life.

Then Moses inadvertently murdered an Egyptian soldier and had to flee into the surrounding desert. Moses spent the second third of his life in the desert of the Midianites. It was here that Moses married and had two sons; most importantly it was in the desert that Moses learned to survive in the wilderness. He would need this experience and expertise for the final third of his life.

Imagine being eighty years old, and being told you were to stand before the most powerful person on earth, and command him to release his entire work force. Imagine that while you are doing this he is seated on a throne, arrayed in regal attire, and surrounded by armed guards. Now picture yourself appearing disheveled, dressed in tattered clothing that smells like sheep and dung. The only thing you have in your hand with which to defend yourself with is a shepherd's staff. Imagine your message to this ostentatious ruler was that you were called to deliver hundreds of thousands of people from his hand of tyranny. Neither he nor the people you are called to deliver give any credence to your words.

This is how the last third of Moses' life began. It was the reason for which he was born.

Can you imagine yourself jumping up and down, clapping your hand, and shouting, "Yes! Let's get on with this!"? I can't. Scripture indicates Moses couldn't either. The task was formidable to say the least; beyond human capability. But therein lies the clue. God was not commanding Moses to do this in his own strength, ability, or intelligence. Moses was created to be the vessel through which God would accomplish what appeared to be the impossible.

At first, Moses was rather reluctant to comply with God's mission. Actually, considering the circumstances, I think most of us would have been also. After a short discussion, Moses acquiesced. God did graciously agree to have Aaron, Moses' brother, be his mouthpiece and right hand man. Following many contentious confrontations with Pharaoh, and many miraculous interventions from God, the Hebrews were set free from Egypt and began the journey back to the land of their ancestors.

Their journey led them across the desert, through the Red Sea, and to the base of Mt. Sinai. It took them two and a half months to arrive at this particular destination.[19] During that time God began revealing Himself to the Hebrews as their Provider, Protector, and Miracle Worker.

It was here at the base of Mt. Sinai that God had the Hebrews momentarily cease their travel and set up camp. This was the place He had chosen for their rest. It was also the place He had chosen to speak to them and instruct them in His ways. His desire was to be in relationship with them. It was here He taught them what He required of them, how to worship and obey Him, and how to live a holy life. It was here He impressed upon them the necessity to be separated unto Him, so that His people would be known as a chosen people, set apart from the rest of humanity.

The Hebrews, who are also known as the Israelites, camped at the foot of Mt. Sinai. This is where we too are going to camp for a while. Just not for the two years that they did.[20]

Up to this point, the journey might be described as long, hot, hard, and full of grumbling and complaining on the part of the people. It did not take the Israelites long to forget the incredible miracles God had performed on their behalf. He had sent unprecedented plagues to the Egyptians which crippled them and forced them to release the Hebrews. He had opened the Red Sea so the Hebrews walked across a path of dry land to safety on the other side. Yet he violently closed that same sea over the chariots and army of Pharaoh, so the Israelites would know that He, and He alone, was Lord. He allowed them to witness with their own eyes the utter destruction of the ones who had kept them in bondage. He caused a rock to gush forth with enough water for all to drink to their satisfaction. He provided food in the form of quail and manna that all might eat to their full. He enabled them to defeat the army of the

Amalekites, even though the Israelites had no weapons and were skilled only in slavery, not warfare.

All of us experience God's miracles every day. Some of them become so commonplace we take them for granted. In most areas of the world we go to bed every night not questioning whether the sun will rise in the morning. And we go throughout our day not giving a second thought to whether it will set in the evening. It's the norm; it's natural. It happens day after day after day.

But if you have ever witnessed the peeking of the sun over the eastern horizon at the break of dawn, breaking forth in rays of pink, red, yellow, and orange as it pierces the darkness with beams of light, you know it is anything but commonplace. And if you have ever witnessed the bowing of the sun behind the western horizon, almost as if signing its name at the end of the day, you know it is anything but ordinary. Each sunrise and each sunset is unique and awesomely magnificent. No two are alike, as if God overlays each morning and each evening with a creative paintbrush that shouts His majesty.

There are many other miracles throughout each day that each one of us experiences. The list is exhaustive. Some of us have experienced unique and personal miracles that have touched our lives in profound and life transforming ways. But there are few of us who have experienced the magnitude of miracles that God showered upon the Israelites again and again and again.

Yet Scripture reveals to us that their short term memory was not so good. Even though they witnessed the miracles with their very own eyes, it wasn't long before they doubted God's goodness, challenged His intentions, grumbled about their conditions, and complained incessantly.

Wayward and unappreciative hearts were nothing new to the Israelites. But Exodus chapter thirty-two relates a particularly disparaging commentary on their attitude, behavior and faith:

When the people saw that Moses was so long in coming down the mountain, they gathered around Aaron and said, "Come, make us gods who will go before us. As for this fellow Moses who brought us up out of Egypt, we don't know what has happened to him."[21]

God had called Moses to the top of Mt. Sinai to meet with Him and give Moses the Ten Commandments. The people had remained at the foot of the mountain. Each tribe was appointed a specific place at which to camp. God had instructed that a barrier be constructed around the base of the mountain so no one would approach the mountain too closely.

Moses had been gone a long time – forty days. He had been gone almost one-half the time it had taken the people to journey from Egypt to Mt. Sinai. While Moses was at the top of the mountain experiencing an incredibly and intensely holy moment with the Almighty, the people were at the bottom of the mountain becoming restless, agitated, and disgruntled. They began to question whether Moses had abandoned them. They began to question whether God had abandoned them. Worse yet, they began to question whether He even really existed.

The people approached Aaron, Moses' brother and God appointed right hand man. They wanted him to produce a god for them. Aaron instructed them to provide him with gold from which he made a golden calf. He then encouraged the people to bow down to the calf and worship it. He had them present it with offerings, and indulge in revelry.

As we view this scene through the lens of history, we are often quick to judge, condemn, and think, "How stupid could they be? What were they thinking?" No condoning what they did; nevertheless, let's consider some often overlooked factors. We tend to forget this was a people that had just left behind everything familiar; whether it was good or not was not the issue – it was familiar. We tend to forget that they were completely clueless about where they were going or how to get there. Although they had experienced miracle after miracle, the truth is they had been uprooted literally overnight and plopped in the middle of nowhere.

We often forget that this was a people who had lived for hundreds of years in a pagan society that worshiped idols, including cows. We tend to forget that perhaps the influence of Egypt was deeply ingrained in their minds, and that they had only been away from that influence for three months. We forget that four centuries had passed since their ancestors had first come to Egypt. A lot can happen in four centuries. A lot can be forgotten. A lot can change.

We forget there was no printing press at that time, so there were no books, records, Bibles, or teachings that could be passed among the people. We tend to forget that no one had the Holy Spirit living within them to convict or give guidance.

We tend to forget that there was only one in the midst of these million people who heard from God, and he was on the top of the mountain that was not only covered with an ominous thick cloud, but was surrounded by lightning bolts and thunder.[22] He had been up there a very long time. Taking these factors into account might make us a little more compassionate and lenient when judging these wanderers; not that they were right by any measure.

Moses was totally oblivious to what was going on in the camp. He was having a glorious mountain-top experience as he was caught up in his encounter with God. But God saw it all, and His righteous anger was ignited.

In that anger God informed Moses of what the people were doing, and that he was going to destroy them for their sin:

Then the LORD said to Moses, "Go down, because your people, whom you brought up out of Egypt, have become corrupt. They have been quick to turn away from what I commanded them and have made themselves an idol cast in the shape of a calf. They have bowed down to it and sacrificed to it and have said, 'These are your gods, O Israel, who brought you up out of Egypt.'

"I have seen these people," the LORD said to Moses, "and they are a stiff-necked people. Now leave me alone so that my anger may burn against them and that I may destroy them. Then I will make you into a great nation."[23]

Moses knew the people he had been leading across the desert were stiff-necked. They were rebellious. They were contentious. More than enough times they had come to him whining and complaining about one thing or another. More than one time he had cried out to God, "Lord, what am I supposed to do with these people?" More than one time he had reached the point of utter exasperation with them.

It would be easy to understand if Moses' response to God's threats was, "Yes Lord, I agree. They are stiff-necked. They are unappreciative and demanding. They don't deserve Your goodness. They need to be taught a good lesson. They're beyond hope." Such a response would be perfectly understandable and logical.

What if Moses had responded to God in that way?

But he didn't.

But Moses sought the favor of the LORD his God. "O LORD," he said, "why should your anger burn against your people, whom you brought up out of Egypt with great power and a mighty hand? Why should the Egyptians say, 'It was with evil intent that he brought them out, to kill them in the mountains and to wipe them off the face of the earth'? Turn from your fierce anger; relent and do not bring disaster on your people. Remember your servants Abraham, Isaac and Israel, to whom you swore by your own self: 'I will make your descendants as numerous as the stars in the sky and I will give your descendants all this land I promised them, and it will be their inheritance forever. [24]

Just as Abraham had a *kairos* moment, so did Moses. Just as Abraham interceded, so did Moses.

But there was a significant difference between the two situations. In Abraham's case, he prayed for a people whom he did not know and who were outside of God's covenant. But Moses personally knew the people God was threatening to destroy. He had spent months with them. Yes, he was fully aware of their hard heartedness. At times he was the brunt of their accusations and rebellion. But over the months he had personally interacted with them. His life had been interwoven with theirs. Beyond his own relationship with them, they were God's chosen people, children of the covenant, and recipients of the promises.

The Moses who had been timid and reluctant in his first encounter with God, took on a new persona. The Scripture says Moses was the meekest man who ever lived.[25] Meekness is a far cry from weakness. In truth, meekness is anything but weakness. By definition, meekness is great strength under control. Here we see Moses demonstrate boldness tempered by humility, and strength tempered by control.

Moses responded to the threat of destruction with meekness and with resolve. He addressed every point God made and turned it around. First, Moses gave the people back to God. God had called them Moses' people, but Moses reminded God that they were not his, but God's. God had said that Moses had led them out of Egypt, but Moses reminded God that it was not his leading, but God's. He reminded God that this whole deliverance ordeal had not been Moses' idea, but God's.

Moses' foremost concern was for God's reputation among the nations. He pleaded with God to consider what such an action would look like to the peoples of the world. Like an attorney presenting closing arguments to a jury or a judge, Moses made the case that such action would only provide the Egyptians with ammunition to malign God's Name and character.

It was not as if God had not thought of this possibility, or had even forgotten it. God was providing an opportunity for Moses to see the situation through God's perspective. He was allowing Moses to reason beyond human perception, and consider the dilemma in light of Kingdom principles. At one point God said to Moses, "...as surely as I live and as surely as the glory of the LORD fills the whole earth..."[26] Moses prayed with the understanding that God's glory throughout the earth was of primary importance.

This was another difference from the prayer of Abraham. Abraham asked God to withhold destruction for the sake of the righteous people that might be living in Sodom and Gomorrah. Moses recognized there was no righteousness of man to rely on, but instead he appealed to the righteousness of God.

Next, Moses instructed God to turn from His fierce anger and relent of His intentions. Pause and ponder this for a moment. What kind of fervor, what kind of passion, and what kind of conviction does it take for **anyone** to instruct God to do **anything**? Moses was either being extremely presumptuous and audacious, or he spoke from a position of influence with confidence in the character of his God.

The culmination of his appeal was to remind God of His promises to Abraham and the patriarchs, to make their descendants numerous and to give to them an inheritance. It was not that God needed to be reminded of the covenant and promises. It was that Moses needed to firmly stand in faith upon them.

An amazing sentence follows the end of Moses' prayer:

Then the LORD relented and did not bring on his people the disaster he had threatened.[27]

Moses' prayer had not been long, but it had been powerful. It was not the length that caught the heart of God, but the strength of Moses' faith behind the prayer.

Can we even begin to imagine the immense relief and gratitude that must have flooded Moses' being when God honored his request to withhold judgement and destruction from the people? Have you ever had a child or someone you love stand before a judge or jury who had the power to convict or absolve them from punishment or imprisonment? Have you ever watched such a scenario on television or the movies? Can you either personally or vicariously identify with the rush of exuberant release felt when a "not guilty" verdict is pronounced? It is like a wave of intense joy and relief pulsating through your body.

With that great news, Moses began down the mountain. As he neared the bottom he heard with his own ears what God had heard all along. He saw with his own eyes what God had seen all along.

Imagine the repulsion that must have welled up within Moses' spirit and soul. He had just left the Presence of the Almighty. He held in his arms the tablets upon which God had written His commandments. There before him, the people he had just interceded for were engaging in all kinds of revelry. There before him, the people bowed down to a golden calf that was raised up in the center of the camp. There before him the people were throwing their treasures towards the golden image and lifting their voices in worship to this false god. Moses' heart must have sank as the heaviness of the moment became a reality to him. Then he discovered it was his very own brother that had initiated the plan. Disbelief, betrayal, regret, anger, revulsion, and fury replaced the feelings of awe and reverence he had experienced just a few moments prior.

This should have been a joyous occasion. This should have been when Moses and his people were reunited following his time apart. This should have been when Moses shared with them the instructions God had given them. This should have been a monumental milestone in their new relationship with the Lord God Almighty.

But it was not. Grievous sin had destroyed the homecoming. Moses, too, now burned with anger. He flung the tablets of stone to the ground, where they shattered in pieces. He destroyed the golden calf by burning it and grinding it to powder. He confronted Aaron and the people with their sin. That day three thousand people died. Division, mourning, grief, anger, and confusion filled the camp.

Moses once again went before the Lord. This time he had seen the sin with his own eyes. This time he had seen the sin as God saw it. This time he understood the offense with Kingdom understanding. This time there was an awareness of the scriptural principle that says godly sorrow leads to repentance.[28]

That is exactly what it did for Moses. He repented on behalf of his people and pleaded for God's forgiveness of their sin. He offered his own name be blotted out from God's book. He was willing to make the ultimate exchange – his life for theirs. His heart was earnest. In this moment he was a foreshadowing of Christ Jesus, for on the cross Christ purchased our forgiveness by taking our sin upon Himself.

So many places along the way this story could have turned out differently.

What if the Israelites had remembered and rehearsed the promises and miracles of God? **What if** they had reminded one another of His goodness and blessings? **What if** His constant protection, provision, and Presence with them was at the forefront of their thinking?

They would have saved themselves an awful lot of heartache.

What if we were faithful in rehearsing and reminding ourselves of the goodness, promises, and miracles of God? **What if** we were faithful to flesh out Philippians 4:8 that says:

Finally brothers, whatever is true, whatever is noble, whatever is right, whatever is pure, whatever is lovely, whatever is admirable – if anything is excellent or praiseworthy – think about such things.

What if we were faithful in reminding each other of such things? **What if** our conversations were filled with the truths of God's living Word? **What if** we encouraged one another as we walk our journey on planet Earth together? **What if** we helped one another through trials, crises, and just ordinary daily living by proclaiming God's goodness? **What if** our hearts and minds were so filled with thanksgiving for all that God has done that praise just naturally and constantly spilled forth from our lips?

The world would be a much more pleasant place to live. God would be recognized as the center and source of all things. We would give no room for our enemy to gain a foothold.

What if the Israelites had not given access to the enemy? **What if** they had not allowed a spirit of discontent to rule their hearts? **What if** they had not engaged in massive grumbling and complaining? **What if** they had not fed the monster of ungratefulness with their words and their actions?

They would have saved themselves an awful lot of heartache.

There is a culture of negativity running rampant in our society today. Criticism, complaining, fault-finding, and blaming are prevalent everywhere. They are destructive to individuals, relationships, communities, the Church, our nation, and the world as a whole. The rise of social media has given new venue to the spewing of hatred, prejudice, and bullying. Just as this did not end well for the Israelites, neither will it end well for us, or any society that yields to the spirit of ungratefulness and the fruit it bears.

What if each one of us purposed in our hearts to wage war against the spirit of negativity? **What if** each one of us determined not to entertain destructive and critical thoughts? **What if** we ceased the judgements against those who are different from us? **What if** we put a halt to grumbling and complaining? **What if** we allowed a sense of contentment to evict the discontent that dwells in our hearts? **What if** we resolved that our words be seasoned with kindness? **What if** each one of us intentionally invited an attitude of gratitude to guide our thinking? **What if** we had the reputation of being a positive and uplifting people, who found good in all things?

We would be so different. And the world would be so different. Anger, anxiety, fear and depression would be on the decline instead of increase. There would probably be fewer people both in prison and therapy. The divorce rate would drop dramatically. Mistrust and divisions on every level would decrease. Perhaps even government and world affairs would be positively impacted.

Just as with the Israelites, the power to choose what will fill our hearts, minds, words, and actions is ours. That power of choice results in a power of influence on those around us. In this way we truly do hold the power to change the world.

Lord, may we choose wisely.

What if Aaron had resisted the people's demands to make them a god? Aaron had been part of the "inner circle." He had not only witnessed the miracles of God, he had been instrumental in each one. **What if** he had held fast to his faith and his convictions?

Then God would have honored Aaron before the people. Then Aaron would have had the satisfaction of knowing he had stood firm and done right in the eyes of the Lord. Then the people would not have gone astray and committed idolatry. Then the children of Israel would have known victory over temptation.

Although the scene at the bottom of Mt. Sinai might seem foreign to us, the truth is, it is way too familiar. Daily we are tempted to turn away from principles we know to be holy and true. Daily we are enticed to compromise our faith and convictions. Daily we are confronted with idols of all kinds. Those idols may differ for each one of us, but the lure to put anything above our worship of God is ever present. There is nothing inherently wrong with possessions, wealth, sports, fame, education, position, television, and numerous other things. But if we allow our pursuit of these things, our time spent in them, or the satisfaction we receive from them to become more important to us than God, they in essence have become idols in our hearts.

What if we committed to truly put God above all things? **What if** we recognized the idols that compete for our affection, allegiance, and attention? **What if** we were able to put them in their proper place and priority? God does not require us to rid ourselves of pleasure and enjoyment. He never said to seek **only** the Kingdom of God. But Jesus did say to seek it **first.**

What if we recognized the influence of peer pressure in our lives to do wrong? **What if** we were not so driven by people pleasing? **What if** we stood firm in our faith in every circumstance, at every crossroad? **What if** we knew God's truth so well that we instantly detected falsehood? **What if** we asked God for the spirit of discernment so that we could identify deception? **What if** we did not allow that deception, no matter how appealing it might be, to lead us astray? **What if** we purposed in our hearts to not be swayed or moved off the foundation of the written and living Word? **What if** we adhered to the One, True, Living, Sovereign, Almighty and Everlasting God, and Him alone?

What we are talking about is choices – such a simple, yet powerful, word. We all face choices every day. Some are big; some are small. Some are insignificant; some have enduring consequences. Some affect only us; and some have far reaching rippling effects. We don't necessarily have to be a leader, as Aaron was, for our choices to either positively or negatively impact the lives of others.

What if Aaron had used his position and influence for good instead of evil? **What if**, as a leader, he had rejected the idea of other gods? **What if** he had spoken words of encouragement to the people? **What if** he had taught them, reminded them, and called them to persevere? **What if**, instead of casting a golden calf, Aaron had led the people in a worship service to the One True God? **What if** he had demonstrated his faith to them in not just words, but by his own behavior and lifestyle?

Aaron would have saved himself, and the people, an awful lot of heartache.

Even though we may not be aware of it, all of us have a circle of influence. For some that circle may be very large. For some it might just be a few. It is not the size of the circle that is significant. The importance lies in how we choose to administer our influence – for good, or for not so good. **What if** we became acutely aware of those we are influencing? **What if** we evaluated the effect of our influence upon others? **What if** we embraced every opportunity of influence given us to bring glory to God? **What if** we intentionally sought out such opportunities? **What if** the mark we left on others' lives was to bring them closer to Jesus? The Scripture says we living epistles, read by all men.[29] **What if** we lived our lives in a manner that the reading pointed those around us to the Kingdom of God?

Lord, may it be so.

After the calf was presented to the Israelites, **what if** they had come to their senses and rejected the idol? **What if** they had had an "ah-ha" moment and reversed their intentions? **What if** they had remembered that the gods of Egypt had been dethroned in the Presence of the God of Israel? **What if** someone, anyone, had stepped forth and rebuked the revelry?

They would have saved themselves an awful lot of heartache.

There is probably a point in all of our lives that we come to the realization that we have allowed idols to creep in and lead us astray. For some of us we might be able to identify many such times. For some of us there might be times in the future we will be convicted. It is how we respond to that conviction that is of paramount importance. **What if** we yield to the prodding of the Holy Spirit? **What if** we humble ourselves before the Lord and seek His forgiveness for a divided heart? **What if** we allow the Holy Spirit to sever the hold those idols might have on us? **What if** we are diligent in doing whatever is necessary to diminish or eradicate their importance to us? **What if** we chose to turn our backs on them and walk away? **What if** we submit ourselves to being accountable to others regarding these things?

The Scripture says:

No temptation has seized you except what is common to man. And God is faithful; he will not let you be tempted beyond what you can bear. But when you are tempted, he will also provide a way out so that you can stand up under it.[30]

Whatever temptation we may face, be it the worship of idols or any other thing, God has promised us a way out so that we may firmly stand in unwavering faith. **What if** we stood upon His promise and rested, trusting Him to do what He says He will do?

What if Moses had not responded to God's threat to destroy the Israelites in the way he had? **What if** he had seen it as a way to rid himself of these bickering, whining, and complaining people? **What if** he had rejoiced in the thought of not having to return to them and put up with them? **What if** he had viewed it as an escape from this monumental task he had not sought in the first place? **What if** he found pleasure in thinking the Lord would honor him and raise a new generation from his seed? **What if** Moses had not cried out for God's mercy and favor on the people? **What if** he had not known the character of God in such a way that he could earnestly appeal to it? **What if** he had not cared for the reputation of God among the nations? **What if** he had not known the promises to Abraham? **What if** he had not known the covenant and therefore could not stand on it? **What if** Moses had not placed himself as a mediator and intercessor between a holy God and a sinful people? **What if** Moses had not cried out in gut-wrenching repentance for the sin of the people – his people, God's people?

The bad news is the results would have been indescribably disastrous and catastrophic.

The good news is Moses did all those things.

We live in a time when the sin of our nation must rise to Heaven and be a stench to God's nostrils. We live in a time when the sins of our nation are far more numerous and far outweigh the sin at Mt. Sinai. We live in a time when there is a desperate need for prayers like the prayer of Moses to be lifted before the Lord.

What if we implored God on behalf of our nation, as Moses did? **What if** we were so completely confident in our position before God, that we could meekly go before Him on behalf of our nation? **What if** we were more concerned for the reputation of God among the nations than we are our own reputation? Aside from Israel, America is the only nation in the world known for its reliance on and adherence to God. America is a nation that was founded upon Judeo/Christian principles. Reference to God is engraved on almost every monument in our nation's Capital. References to the Almighty are found in many of our founding and historical documents. Missionaries have been sent forth from America to bring the Gospel of Christ throughout the world. America has been open-handed to meet the needs of the less fortunate throughout the world. America has been a light of hope in dark times. She has been a fortress of safety to those in distress. All of this is not because America is great, but because the God she serves is great. **What if** in our prayers we could rehearse these things and say, "God surely, You will protect this nation that trusts in You, that honors You, that was founded upon Your truth, and

61

that preaches Your Name. Surely, Lord, You do not want the pagan nations of the world to proclaim You have turned Your back on the people called by Your Name. Surely You do not want them to think You are not loving enough to forgive, or powerful enough to save, or compassionate enough to have mercy."

What if we would pray for our nation standing on the promises of old, seeking His will, and adhering to the covenant?

What if we would come before the Lord in genuine repentance, bringing every sin before Him, crying out for His forgiveness?

Do you think it would make a difference? I do.

Lord, may it be so.

Finally, **what if** God had not relented in His plan to destroy the people? **What if** He had rejected Moses' heartfelt appeal? **What if** He had acted upon His anger? **What if** the intercession of Moses had fallen on deaf ears?

The amazing thing is that God did relent; He did accept Moses' appeal; He did not act in anger, and He heard the genuine cry of Moses' heart.

This story in Numbers 32 shows us, that in a sense, we can change the mind of God. We serve a God whose character, holiness, and purpose never change. But – and this is a big **but** – He is willing to change His actions in response to our prayers and intercessions. He is the same yesterday, today and forever,[31] but His warnings and promises are conditional. On what are they conditional? They are conditional on us, and our responses to Him. God is still looking for those who will hunger for His voice, who will seek a "now" word, who will come before Him in meekness, and who will intercede for our nation as Moses interceded for the children of Israel.

Father God, would You raise up intercessors all across this land who will labor in prayer on behalf of our nation? Will You raise up a remnant who will contend for Your truth, Your principles, and Your ways to once again reign in our nation? Would You raise up men and women who have the meekness of Moses to boldly stand for what is right and true? Would you raise up servants with the heart of Moses who care about Your reputation throughout the nations? Would You forgive us of our sins, our idolatry, our rebellious nature, and our ungratefulness? Will You hold Your banner of righteousness over our nation? May we proclaim and reflect Your greatness for all to see. In Jesus' Name, Amen.

PERSONAL REFLECTION

1. As you look back over your life, can you identify seasons where God was preparing you for something in the future? How did He accomplish the preparation? Did you resist or co-operate?

2 .What have you found to be the fruit of a negative or ungrateful spirit? Can you identify specific times in your life? If you could rewind the tape, what would you do differently?

3. How has peer pressure affected your life or walk with the Lord? Are there certain situations that stand out to you more than others? What did you learn from these times?

4. Can you identify idols you have had, or even still have? What will you do about them?

6. What three **what ifs** spoke to you the most? Would you add any?

5
A MAN AFTER THE HEART OF GOD
II Samuel 7; I Chronicles 17

A long time had passed since the incident at Mt. Sinai. After forty grueling years, the children of Israel finally made it to their destination. Those years were filled with many more occasions of rebellion and dissonance. Only two who were of age when they left the bondage of Egypt made it to the Promised Land – Caleb and Joshua. God honored the steadfast faith these two men had exhibited in the midst of massive and continual doubt from others. They were among the remnant that would possess God's promises. All of the others, including Moses and Aaron, had died somewhere in the wilderness.

God had appointed Joshua to lead the people across the Jordan River and into the Promised Land, also known as Israel. Once in the land of their ancestors, the cycle of disobedience did not stop. There were periods of faithfulness, although these were generally short lived. There were periods of victory. There were periods of warfare. There were periods of failure and defeat. There were periods of waywardness. Judges 21:25 describes these as times when each person did what was right in their own eyes. God raised up judges, prophets, and eventually a king to lead the people. It was not an easy assignment for any of them.

And then God set His holy eyes upon a young shepherd boy whose heart blessed the heart of God. David was the eighth born son to a man named Jesse. As the youngest, one can imagine David was the recipient of much "brotherly abuse". In fact, the Scripture gives us glimpses into how the seven older siblings mocked and ridiculed their "baby" brother.

As with Moses, God not only set His eyes, but also His hand on this young lad. God ministered to David as he was alone in the fields or on the mountains with his sheep. He watched over David and enabled him to be a fierce protector of his flocks. Often God uses the most unseemly places to accomplish His purposes. Whether in the sheep pen or the green pastures, God was training David to be a shepherd of people, a defender, a warrior, and a leader.

God instructed the prophet Samuel to commission and anoint David, while he was still a youth, to be king over all of Israel. David did not actually ascend to the throne for many years. The time in-between was preparation time, and the going was not easy. David probably questioned the reality of his kingship many times, for the path God laid before him looked nothing like the typical path of royalty.

Imagine how David must have felt when the current king, Saul, accused him of betrayal and treason. Imagine what he must have experienced when his intentions, motives, and character were challenged and criticized. Imagine being at the mercy of the one person who could authorize your death. Imagine your best friend and confidant being the son of the one who desired your demise. Imagine how David must have felt being hunted down like an animal by Saul and his army. Imagine knowing you were to be king, but living in caves and struggling for your very existence. This was David's passageway to the throne.

Have you ever experienced a similar path? Have you ever believed with your whole being that you were supposed to accomplish a certain task, yet circumstances seemed to lead you in a totally different direction? Have you ever felt like you make one step forward and two steps back? Have unexpected situations arisen that divert you away from what would be logical and normal? Have you ever begun to question the reality of the call, or the possibility of it ever happening? Have you ever become disheartened and discouraged? David's path looked like it led anywhere but to the throne. And that path was orchestrated by God. God was more concerned about the character He was building in David than He was in the destination. That is always true in our lives also. We focus on the destination; God delights in the journey and what He accomplishes in us through that journey. Perhaps some things can be accomplished no other way.

In God's perfect timing, David became king over first Judea, and then all of Israel. The period of David's reign is referred to as the "Golden Age" in Jewish history. David was renowned as a mighty and victorious warrior, conquering every enemy he faced. But he was equally renowned as a man with a heart that was zealous and passionate for his God.

David was a man's man. He was skilled in all kinds of battle and all manner of warfare. He was also a ladies' man, which, at times, ensnared him in more trouble than he wanted. But mostly he was God's man. Scripture refers to him as "a man after God's own heart."

One of the very first things David set his mind to do after being anointed king was to bring the Ark of the Covenant to Jerusalem. Years earlier, during a period referred to as the time of the Judges, the Ark of the Covenant had been captured by the Philistine army and taken from the Israelites. Why was this significant? Because God had told the Israelites while they were still in the desert under the leadership of Moses, that He dwelt between the wings of the cherubim on the Ark of the Covenant. Inside the Ark were the stone tablets that contained the Ten Commandments. The Ark of the Covenant was the holiest symbol Israel had of God.

The Ark had been absent from the land of Israel for about forty years. During this lapse of time no one else even attempted to recapture it and return it to its rightful place. No one even seemed to think it important. All that changed when David became king. The Ark in itself was simply an ornate box with no supernatural power, but to David it was symbolic of God's Presence with His people. David was one who could not live his life or rule his nation without the Presence.

In Psalm 27:4 David says:

One thing I ask of the LORD, this is what I seek: That I may dwell in the house of the LORD all the days of my life, To gaze upon the beauty of the LORD and to seek him in his temple.

Bringing the Ark of the Lord to Jerusalem was not an easy endeavor. David assembled an extravagant procession of elders, priests, and worshipers to accompany the Ark on the journey.[32] The directions God gave had to be followed explicitly. To veer from them could, and in one instance actually did, end in death.[33] It was costly in other ways also. When the priests who were carrying the Ark took six steps, the procession would stop. Then they would sacrifice a fattened bull and calf.[34] It must have been a very bloody trail. It also cost David his relationship with his wife, Michal, as she disdained and criticized David for his uninhibited worship.[35]

What if we had the kind of passion for God that David had? **What if** the deepest longing of our hearts was to be in His Presence? **What if** our desire was to pour extravagant love upon Him? **What if** we didn't count the costs? **What if** we persevered to overcome any and all barriers to pursue Him?

What if He alone was our "one thing?" **What if** we actually did love Him with all our heart, and all our mind, and all our being? **What if** we sought Him with reckless abandon?

David did, and the burning desire of his heart was to seek and bask in the Presence of the Lord. He not only succeeded in bringing the Ark back to Jerusalem, but he erected a tent in which the Ark was housed. He established that continual worship, sacrifices, and prayer be conducted within the tent by regiments of priests, day and night, without interruption. Some believe David had this tent pitched near his own palace so he could always be near God's Presence.

David's entire life was a life of prayer. The book of Psalms is evidence of that. Whether David was in a place of despair, a place of victory, or a place of prophetic worship, the Psalms show that God was the One to Whom he ran and to Whom he poured out his heart. Whether he was in distress or experiencing exhilaration; whether he was in a place of repentance or exuberant thanksgiving, David's habit was to turn to God.

Entire books have been written on the many prayers of David. Here, however, we are going to focus on the one found in both II Samuel 7, and I Chronicles 17.

"Who am I, O LORD God, and what is my family, that you have brought me this far? And as if this were not enough in your sight, O God, you have spoken about the future of the house of your servant. You have looked on me as though I were the most exalted of men, O LORD God.

"What more can David say to you for honoring your servant? For you know your servant, O LORD. For the sake of your servant and according to your will, you have done this great thing and made known all these great promises.

"There is no one like you, O LORD, and there is no God but you, as we have heard with our own ears. And who is like

your people Israel – the one nation on earth whose God went out to redeem a people for himself, and to make a name for yourself, and to perform great and awesome wonders by driving out nations from before your people, whom you redeemed from Egypt? You made your people Israel your very own forever, and you, O LORD, have become their God.

"And now, LORD, let the promise you have made concerning your servant and his house be established forever. Do as you promised, so that it will be established and that your name will be great forever. Then men will say, 'The LORD Almighty, the God over Israel, is Israel's God!' And the house of your servant David will be established before you.

"You, my God, have revealed to your servant that you will build a house for him. So your servant has found courage to pray to you. O LORD, you are God! You have promised these good things to your servant. Now you have been pleased to bless the house of your servant, that it may continue forever in your sight; for you, O LORD, have blessed it, and it will be blessed forever."

Scholars are not sure exactly when David prayed this prayer. We do, however, know the circumstances around it. David must have reigned over both Judea and Israel for several years. Many battles with foreign nations had been fought and won. II Samuel 7 begins with, *"After the king was settled in his palace and the LORD had given him rest from all his enemies around him..."* Two pieces of information are given in that short opening: that enough time had gone by during which a palace could be erected; that David was enjoying a time of peace, as all his enemies had been defeated.

It was during this time, when David was probably resting in his palace and gazing upon the tent in which the Ark was housed, that he came up with an idea. Why should he live in a beautifully adorned house, while the Ark of the Covenant was in a simple and humble tent? Was it not selfish and irreverent that he should have built himself a magnificent home, while he had provided for God only a tent?

I imagine these initial questions grew into thoughts that consumed David day and night. I imagine he began to envision a more suitable house in which the Lord could dwell. I imagine such thoughts excited him. I imagine he experienced much pleasure and great anticipation from the planning. This was "his baby," so to speak, and was an expression of his devotion to His God. No one had ever attempted such a thing.

Eventually David could not contain these thoughts. He summoned the prophet Nathan to inform him of his plans. Initially Nathan gave his consent. This, however, was before he had sought or heard from the Lord. Perhaps it seemed like a "no-brainer" to both David and Nathan. Perhaps they thought there was no need to consult the Lord. This was such an outstanding idea, how or why would God possibly disagree?

But He did. That night, God told Nathan to tell David, "No." The message was full of grace and gentleness, but the bottom line was that David was not to build a house for the Lord.

Stop for a moment and think about how this might have felt to David. Have you ever been so excited about the prospect of doing something that it occupies your every thought? Have you ever been ecstatic about an idea you conceived all by yourself? Have you truly believed God had called you to do something? Have you ever experienced the delight of thinking about how you were going to surprise and bless someone else? Have you ever pondered their expression and reaction with that surprise? Have you ever felt the joy of preparing for some kind of ministry? Have you laid awake at night planning, organizing, and making arrangements in your mind? Have you allowed the prospects to thrill your heart? Have you spent time gathering provisions that might be needed? Have you experienced the anticipation of seeing the plans come to fruition?

Then have you ever experienced being told you couldn't do what you had set your heart on? Have you ever felt the pain of having your idea rejected? Have you ever had the door slammed shut on a ministry you were sure was God's purpose for your life? Have you ever known the anguish of having your expression of love turned down? It can be extremely painful and disheartening.

David's response to God is so immediately and overwhelmingly positive, we forget that it could have been very different. David could have sulked, pouted, and thought God was being completely unfair and unjust. His prayer could have been filled with anger, resentment, bargaining, and manipulation. He could have had Nathan thrown out or even killed. He could have accused Nathan of rebellion and sedition. He could have labeled Nathan a false prophet and sentenced him to stoning. He could have forged ahead with his plans, discrediting both the message and the messenger. But he did none of these things.

What do we do when God says "No" to our plans? How do we react? Do we symbolically hold our hands over our ears and say, "I can't hear You!"? Do we try to rationalize that surely God wouldn't be saying "No?" Surely it must be the enemy! Do we try to push through, ignoring whatever obstacles He might put in front of us? Do we talk to others and try to get them to validate our ideas? Do we scheme, connive, and maneuver, trying to prove we are right?

God's message to David through Nathan was not all negative. In His great mercy and grace, He also spoke words of endearment and promise to David regarding the future. Indeed, this helped cushion the blow of the "No." God is the originator of "I've got a better idea".

That's something for us to remember when we receive a "No" from God. He always has a better idea, a better plan. He may not inform us at the time, as He did with David, but it is a matter of His character. He may not act in our timing, but His timing will always be better. He is faithful and will bring to pass the things that are to be accomplished in a much better way than we could ever imagine.

God was blessed by the desire of David's heart, but He had a far greater idea. The house that David desired to build would be built by David's son, Solomon. That in itself must have thrilled David's heart. What parent does not yearn for their children to achieve greater things than they have?

Beyond even that, God's idea was for a different house – one that would affect all eternity and all mankind. The "No" for David turned into a "Yes" for Christ. Instead of David building a house for God, God was going to build a "house" through the line of David that would endure forever. The "house" God was referring to was the Messiah who would come through the bloodline of David, and the Church that would be His bride.

This was indeed exceptional, excellent, and wondrous news! But if David's heart had not been softened and right before God, I imagine he could have gotten stuck at the "No" and never realized the magnificence of the promise.

We do that sometimes. Sometimes we get so stuck in the "No" that we miss the promises and possibilities. Sometimes not getting our way causes our ears to be dulled, our vision to be blurry, and our heart to be full of ugly junk. Sometimes we get our spiritual feathers ruffled and have unholy temper tantrums.

The words of David's prayer upon hearing the message from Nathan reflect a heart of humility and gratefulness. David does not question God's decision. He does not refute it, or try to bargain with God to get his way. He totally yields, submits, accepts, rejoices, and exalts his Maker.

What if David had responded differently than he had? **What if** he had resented God's message? **What if** he had become jealous that someone other than himself was chosen to fulfill his plans? **What if** he had denied that such a "No" was from God? **What if** he had forged full steam ahead to build the house?

There were many occasions in David's life when he had to choose which path he would follow – his own, man's, or God's. On some of those occasions David failed, but he always recognized his sin and came to the Lord in repentance. On this occasion, however, he passed with flying colors, and he leaves us with a wonderful example of how to respond to God's "No."

What if we learned from this example David left us? **What if** we too would surrender our desires, plans, and agendas to the will of God and with grateful, humble hearts accept whatever He says? **What if** we focused on His promises more than our disappointments? **What if** we rejoiced that God always has a better idea than we do, no matter how good we think our idea may be? **What if** we rejoiced when God appoints someone else to do what we want to do? **What if** we ceased comparing and thinking we are more qualified than whoever might step into our shoes? **What if** we simply trusted that God knows what He is doing?

David's example applies not only to our personal lives and plans; his example also applies to our nation. **What if** we learned to submit the plans we make as a nation to the will of God? **What if** we stopped considering ourselves too wise and powerful to need His direction? **What if** we realized His ideas are far better than ours? **What if** we learned how to accept His "No" with grace and thanksgiving?

David was not only a lover of God who wanted to provide a suitable house in which God could dwell, he was the king of the nation. Although David had a beautifully personal and intimate relationship with God, David's desire was not just for himself. As king, David realized the importance of God's Presence to the nation. He was fully aware of their need for God's favor upon them. As leader, he knew it was imperative for God to be the center of life and for Him to be honored among the people. Building a place for the Ark to be housed would make God's Presence more accessible to the people. David's desire was not only to bless God, but for His people to be blessed *by* God as they sought to know Him. He wanted them to have a place to go where they might pray, worship, and experience His Presence. David was fully aware that the nation of Israel and her people could not and would not enjoy the blessings God had for them without the Presence of the Almighty in their midst.

Neither can our nation. It is God's Presence with a people that distinguishes them and sets them apart from all other peoples of the earth.[36] Psalm 33:12 says, *"Blessed is the nation whose God is the LORD."* Just as David was mindful of the importance of God's Presence among His people, it is imperative that God's Presence be manifest within our nation today. If America is to maintain her integrity, justice, and solidarity as a nation, she must value and yield to the Presence of the Almighty. If she is to have the umbrella of God's blessings and favor over her, she must acknowledge and desire His Presence in her midst.

What if we prayed daily for the men and women in every level of leadership in our nation? **What if** we persevered in prayer for God to place men and women who have hearts for Him in places of authority? **What if** we asked God to give our leaders the same heart that David had? **What if** our leaders recognized our nation's desperate need for God? **What if** the leaders of our nation today were more concerned about the spiritual condition of their hearts than their reputation? **What if** they were genuinely concerned about the spiritual condition of America and the people within her borders? **What if** they sought the Lord in their decisions? **What if** they recognized that He not only has a better idea, but He has the best idea? **What if** our leaders lived their lives according to God's principles and encouraged the people to do so? **What if** the Presence of God was sought after and revered by men and women in leadership? **What if** they gave more place for God in America by inviting His Presence into their midst, and seeking His guidance and favor upon all the decisions they make?

Holy and Gracious Father, we ask in Jesus' Name that You birth the heart of David in all of us, especially the leaders of America. Cause us to seek You. Cause us to desire You. Cause us to recognize our need for Your Presence and guidance in everything concerning our nation. Cause us as a people, especially our leaders, to call upon You. May they invite and welcome You to take up residency and freely dwell among us. In Jesus' Name, Amen.

PERSONAL REFLECTION

1. Has there been a time in your life when it seemed as if everything was going in the wrong direction? What did you learn during that time?

2. How do you seek the Presence of the Lord? Has it ever cost you anything?

3. Have there been seasons in your walk with Him that have been particularly precious? What do you think made them that way?

4. Have you ever received a "No" from God? How did you handle it? Looking back on it, can you understand why God said "No"? Did He have a better idea?

5. Which three **what ifs** spoke to you the most?

6
THE HOUSE THAT SOLOMON BUILT
I Kings 8; II Chronicles 6

Despite the fact that David was a man after God's own heart, in his humanness he sinned. Despite the fact that he is remembered as a worshipper, there were times he plummeted into the clutches of iniquity. Some of those times the transgression may have been minor; other times the sin was glaring and major. The very nature of leadership places one in the spotlight; the very nature of leadership holds one to a higher standard. A leader often finds themselves living in a fish bowl where their behavior is visible for scrutiny. So it was for David.

At one point in his life, David succumbed to the spirit of lust and committed adultery with a married woman. As if this was not unscrupulous enough, he arranged for the death of her husband because she had become pregnant from the affair. After some time, Nathan the prophet, confronted David with his sin. Although there are many lessons we can glean from David's offense, there are equally important ones we can learn from how he handled it once it was exposed.

David could have had Nathan killed because of the accusation he brought against the king. David could have raged and denied the events. He could have accused Nathan of treason. He did none of those things. Instead, he immediately confessed that he had sinned against the Lord.[37] David, the king, quickly acknowledged his sin. The next words out of Nathan's mouth were, *"The LORD has taken away your sin."*[38]

There is something very precious about that transaction. There is something precious about the brevity of it. Once exposed, David wasted no time before he accepted the responsibility of his iniquity. Once he accepted it, God wasted no time before He forgave.

God's forgiveness is wonderful, but it does not always exempt us from the consequences of our sin. Nathan also had to deliver a word of consequence to David. The child that had been conceived and was born through the adulterous affair would die.[39]

Upon hearing this, David fasted, prostrated himself on the floor, and prayed. He did not get up, he did not eat, and he did not stop praying for seven days. On the seventh day the child died.

We might view this as a horrible punishment from the Lord. We might interpret this as an unfair and extreme penalty to pay. Could it be that God saw it differently and that His intentions were for good?

If the child had lived, every time David looked upon him he might have been reminded of his sin. The very presence of the child might have brought remorse to David's soul as he thought about his transgression. God told David He had taken away his sin. He also took away the fruit of that sin. He removed the reminder of that sin. God's cleansing was not partial, but complete. So it is with us. When God forgives us He does not want us to continue dwelling on our sin. He does not want us to live under the bondage of regret, guilt, and condemnation.

There are many stories in the Old Testament that are repeated at least once, if not several times. The story of the exodus from Egypt under Moses is retold many times throughout Scripture. The two books of Chronicles contain the same stories that are in the two books of Kings. Many of the stories of David that are in First and Second Samuel are repeated in First Chronicles.

The story of David's sin of adultery is told only once. It is found in II Samuel 11. It is told, but it is never repeated. Not another mention or a reference to it will be found throughout Scripture. It is recorded because it happened. But it is not repeated, because it was forgiven. David learned his lesson, confessed, and repented. God took his sin away. *Done; over; forgotten; end of story; not to be brought up again.*

So it is when we genuinely repent. God forgives.

But the child's death was not the end of the story. What transpired between David and God as he fasted, lay on that floor, and prayed for seven days, we do not know. That, too, is precious. That was an intimate time between David and his God. That was a time when David must have poured out his heart. It was a time of working through his deep emotions. It has stayed strictly between David and God all these years.

Can you recall a time when you were undone with grief because of a sin you had committed? Can you remember going before the Lord and pouring out your soul? Can you remember pleading for His forgiveness? Do you remember the sweetness of His acceptance of your repentance? Do you remember the tenderness with which He assured you of His love? Has God ever brought it up to you again? Has God ever exposed your sin to those around you? Or, as your safe hiding place, has He kept it between you and Him, just as He did with David? Has He covered you with His mercy that keeps away what we do deserve? Has He covered you with His grace that gives us what we don't deserve?

All Scripture is inspired by God[40] and He could put anything He wants in His Word. He has revealed things about individuals and mankind that are unpleasant, appalling, and horrific. There have been times that He used the prophets to call peoples and nations out for their vile behavior. There have been times He has not minced words. There have been times He left no doubt as to His displeasure. He could have recorded every word spoken between David and God for all mankind and all generations to see.

But God didn't. He held the intimate exchange between David and Himself close to His heart. It was a matter of respect and confidentiality. He does the same thing with each of us. He listens as we pour out our deepest desires and tenderly holds each word with protected privacy. He is the revealer of secrets and hidden things; *but they are His secrets, not ours.* No one else is privy to our intimate times with Him. It is a holy exchange between the loved and the beloved.

It appears however, that David was strengthened by this time with the Lord. It appears that he received the "mind of Christ"[41] as he prayed, for when he was finished those around him were surprised by his countenance, peace, and acceptance.

The child did die, just as the prophet said.[42] Then God in His great and bountiful mercy allowed another child to be born to David and the woman, who had become David's wife. God is not a God who delights in taking away. He is a God who delights in giving. God is not a God who delights in punishing, but a God who delights in blessing. God is a God that brings life where there has been death. He is a God of new beginnings and second chances.

God greatly loved this son born to David. God named him Jedidiah which means "loved by God." His parents named him Solomon which means "peace." He indeed was a gift from God who brought peace to their aching hearts.

Solomon was not the firstborn of David, nor the second, nor the third. Normally, the position of king was passed down to sons according to the birth order. According to I Chronicles 3, Solomon may have been the eighth or ninth son born to David, and therefore not in line for the throne. But God's hand and favor were upon Solomon from his conception, and God appointed him to reign over Israel after David's death.

David spent much time instructing Solomon not only in the ways of kingship, but especially in the construction of the temple. God had been pleased with David's desire to build a house for Him, but had not allowed David to build it because he was a man of war. David accepted God's decision, but that did not hinder him from preparing, planning, and gathering materials for the temple. In his later years, David shared all of his insights and preparations with Solomon. He impressed upon him the magnitude and importance of the task.[43]

Upon David's death, Solomon was anointed and crowned king over Israel, just as the prophet Nathan had said. In the fourth year of his reign, he began the massive undertaking of constructing the temple, a house in which God, who cannot be contained, could dwell. It took approximately seven years to complete the work.[44] The temple was a magnificent and palatial structure, created with the finest and most costly materials. It was both splendid and breathtaking to behold.

It was fitting that the dedication of the temple was during the festival of the seventh month, the Feast of Tabernacles.[45] This feast was the last of seven feasts required by God for the Israelites to celebrate during the Jewish calendar year. God had given the instructions for each feast through Moses before the Israelites entered the Promised Land. This particular feast was to be celebrated for a week, and was one of great joy and festivity. The people were to build shelters of various branches and leaves and commemorate God's Presence with them throughout their wilderness experience. It was also prophetic of the coming of Christ, as He would one day tabernacle, or dwell with His people. The prophet Zechariah spoke of a future day when the Lord will reign from the throne of David in Jerusalem. During that time, the Feast of Tabernacles will be celebrated as once again God will tabernacle with mankind.[46]

As the priests placed the Ark of the Covenant in the Most Holy Place, a thick cloud filled the temple as the glory of the Lord descended. The Presence of God was taking up residency with His people. The outward appearance of the temple was indeed splendid and breathtaking, but the Shekinah glory of God that filled the inner sanctum was far beyond that by any measure of comparison.

It was at this time that King Solomon spread out his hands and lifted up a prayer of dedication before the people and to the Lord. It is the longest and most detailed prayer spoken by man in the Bible.

"O LORD, God of Israel, there is no God like you in heaven or on earth – you who keep your covenant of love with your servants who continue wholeheartedly in your way. You have kept your promise to your servant David my father; with

your mouth you have promised and with your hand you have fulfilled it – as it is today.

"Now LORD, God of Israel, keep for your servant David my father the promises you made to him when you said, 'You shall never fail to have a man to sit before me on the throne of Israel, if only your sons are careful in all they do to walk before me according to my law, as you have done.' And now, O LORD, God of Israel, let your word that you promised your servant David come true.

"But will God really dwell on earth with men? The heavens, even the highest heavens, cannot contain you. How much less this temple I have built! Yet give attention to your servant's prayer and his plea for mercy, O LORD my God. Hear the cry and the prayer that your servant is praying in your presence. May your eyes be open toward this temple day and night, this place which you said you would put your Name there. May you hear the prayer your servant prays toward this place. Hear the supplications of your servant and of your people Israel when they pray toward this place. Hear from heaven, your dwelling place, and when you hear, forgive.

"When a man wrongs his neighbor and is required to take an oath and he comes and swears the oath before your altar in this temple, then hear from heaven and act. Judge between your servants, repaying the guilty by bringing down on his own head what he has done. Declare the innocent not guilty and so establish his innocence.

"When your people Israel have been defeated by an enemy because they have sinned against you and when they turn back and confess your name, praying and making supplication before you in this temple, then hear from heaven and forgive the sin of your people Israel and bring them back to the land you gave to them and their fathers.

"When the heavens are shut up and there is no rain because your people have sinned against you, and when they pray toward this place ad confess your name and turn from their sin because you have afflicted them, then hear from heaven and forgive the sin of your servants, your people Israel. Teach them the right way to live, and send rain on the land you gave your people for an inheritance.

"When famine or plague comes to the land, or blight or mildew, locusts or grasshoppers, or when enemies besiege them in any of their cities, whatever disaster or disease may come, and when a prayer or plea is made by any of your people Israel – each one aware of his afflictions and pains, and spreading out his hands toward this temple – then hear from heaven, your dwelling place. Forgive, and deal with each man according to all he does, since you know his heart (for you alone know the hearts of men), so that they will fear you and walk in your ways all the time they live in the land you gave our fathers.

"As for the foreigner who does not belong to your people Israel but has come from a distant land because of your great name and your mighty hand and your outstretched arm – when he comes and prays toward this temple, then hear from heaven, your dwelling place, and do whatever the foreigner asks of you, so that all the peoples of the earth may know your name and fear you, as do your own people Israel, and may know that this house I have built bears your Name.

"When your people go to war against their enemies, wherever you send them, and when they pray to you toward this city you have chosen and the temple I have built for your Name, then hear from heaven their prayer and their plea, and uphold their cause.

"When they sin against you – for there is no one who does not sin – and you become angry with them and give them over

to the enemy, who takes them captive to a land far away or near; and if they have a change of heart in the land where they are held captive, and repent and plead with you in the land of their captivity and say, 'We have sinned, we have done wrong and acted wickedly'; and if they turn back to you with all their heart and soul in the land of their captivity where they were taken, and pray toward the land you gave their fathers, toward the city you have chosen and toward the temple I have built for your Name; then from heaven, your dwelling place, hear their prayer and their pleas, and uphold their cause. And forgive your people, who have sinned against you.

"Now, my God, may your eyes be open and your ears attentive to the prayers offered in this place.

"Now arise, O LORD God, and come to your resting place, you and the ark of your might. May your priests, O LORD God, be clothed in salvation, may your saints rejoice in your goodness. O LORD God, do not reject your anointed one. Remember the great love promised to David your servant."[47]

Initially this may appear to be an unusual prayer of dedication, at least by current standards. The tone seems void of celebration; but rather one of somberness. Although quite lengthy, there is minimal focus on the consecration of the temple, and nominal invoking of God's blessings. Instead, Solomon reminds God of His promises to David, and concentrates more on the issues of sin and forgiveness.

The message seems to be neither overly optimistic nor overly pessimistic, but rather that of a pragmatist. Solomon's prayer of dedication on this momentous occasion in Israel's history was certainly not from the perspective of one wearing rose-colored glasses, but it was not entirely doom and gloom either.

What made Solomon such a pragmatist? Maybe he was just one by nature. Perhaps it was from his own personal encounters with temptation. Perhaps observing the sins of his older brothers, and the consequences they suffered, made Solomon keenly aware of the pitfalls of sin. Perhaps it came from being king for eleven years and dealing with the attitude and behavior of his people.

Perhaps it was a result of wisdom. When Solomon first ascended the throne he asked God to give him wisdom to rule the kingdom and its people. God was pleased with Solomon's request and granted it. As his father David, was remembered as "the man after God's own heart," Solomon's was renowned as being "the wisest man who ever lived."[48] His fame went beyond the borders of Israel; leaders from nations far away honored him because of his reputation. Wisdom and pragmatism are valuable assets for those in leadership.

Solomon's prayer was a unique weaving together of former law and prophetic events. Before the Israelites had ever entered the Promised Land, God spoke a series of blessings and curses to the people. They are recorded in Leviticus 26 and Deuteronomy 28. He forewarned the people that if they were disobedient to Him, He would allow certain hardships to come upon them. These hardships would grow in intensity and severity the farther the people strayed and the longer they resisted His discipline. God's purpose was never to harm His people, but to make them aware of their waywardness. Solomon reminded the people of God's warnings within his prayer.

His words were also prophetic in that they spoke of things that would happen in Israel's future. He did not speak as if they might happen, but declared that they would. His words did not imply possibility; they did not even imply probability. They proclaimed with certainty that men would wrong their neighbors, Israel would be defeated by enemies and her people taken captive, the heavens would be shut up, there would be famine, blight, and mildew in the land, foreigners would come to the land, armies would go to war, and people would sin. Tragically, all of these things did come to pass.

In essence, Solomon's prayer of dedication was a uniting of God's forewarned curses with the inevitability of the people's sin, and the consequences they would suffer because of that sin. He viewed with crystal clarity the direct relationship between man's sin and God's discipline. Solomon regarded sin as the root of all man's hardships. He understood that whether God meted out blessings or curses was totally determined by the obedience or disobedience of man.

Perhaps Solomon thought it imperative to remind the people of this, since God would now be inhabiting a house that was in their midst. Perhaps he wanted them to be keenly conscious of the nearness of God as he tabernacled with them. Perhaps he was encouraging them to be mindful of, and accountable for, their behavior, as God's Presence was among them.

Despite his proclamation of discipline to come, Solomon did not leave the people without hope. Despite his continual reference to their propensity to sin, he also reminded them of God's gift of prayer, repentance, and forgiveness. Essentially he was telling them, "No matter how badly you sinned, no matter how far you stray, no matter how severe the situation, you can always cry out for forgiveness."

Solomon concluded this somber prayer with an invitation for God to take up residency within the temple.

The Lord accepted the invitation and tabernacled with His people. It was in His response to Solomon that God spoke these words of promise with which we are so familiar:

"...if my people, who are called by my name, will humble themselves and pray and seek my face and turn from their wicked ways, then will I hear from heaven and will forgive their sin and will heal their land."[49]

What if we had a clearer understanding of the relationship between our sins and the consequences they bring? **What if** we recognized that obedience to the Lord opens the windows of blessing, whereas our sin closes it? **What if** we stopped blaming others for the circumstances in our lives and owned our own responsibility for the things we have done? **What if** we welcomed His discipline, knowing it was for our good? **What if** we responded to that discipline through prayer and repentance? **What if** we recognized our need for His forgiveness? **What if** repentance was a normal way of life for us? **What if** we fully received and embraced His forgiveness? **What if** we recognized the power of forgiveness to set us free and to give us a brand new start?

What if we had leaders who would pray over our nation and its people the way Solomon did? **What if** we had leaders who would seek God for wisdom to govern our country? **What if** we had leaders who cried out for the Presence of God to inhabit every aspect of our existence? **What if** our leaders invited God to inhabit every house of government across our land? **What if** we had leaders who understood the promises and principles of God? **What if** they believed that those promises and principles are as true today as when they were given? **What if** our leaders allowed God's truths to be the foundation from which they governed? **What if** our leaders sought the Lord's vision for our nation? **What if** they chose to see the future through His eyes? **What if** they recognized that the disasters that happen in our nation just might be a result of our sin? **What if** our leaders encouraged us as a nation to pray, repent, and seek God's forgiveness? **What if** they were to model the importance of prayer for our nation?

Although Solomon reigned as king nearly three thousand years ago, the crises he addressed were similar to the ones we face today: natural disasters, wars, famines, injustices. **What if** we were to understand that these are not just happenstance, but a result of our sin? **What if** we allowed them to remind us of our need for God? **What if** we allowed them to draw us back to Him? **What if** we ceased handling them through our own efforts and abilities, but went to the real root of the problem?

What if we understood that today God's Presence does not dwell in a physical building? **What if** we stopped looking for Him in structures made of brick or stone? **What if** we believed that *we* are the tabernacles He has chosen to inhabit? **What if** we realized His Spirit dwells within us? **What if** we were keenly aware that God's Presence is continually with us? **What if** knowing that would help us think twice before we act or speak? **What if** we understood that His Spirit within us gives us power over sin? What if we understood that His Spirit enables us to say "No" to sin?

What if we believed God has the power to heal our land? **What if** we would do more than just quote II Chronicles 7:14? **What if** we would stand upon its promise every day and not just on special occasions during the year? **What if** we were to actually do what it says? **What if** we were to fall on our knees, confess our sins, turn from our wicked ways, and trust Him to answer? **What if** we resolved to be part of the remnant that does not waver, does not compromise, and earnestly seeks God on behalf of our nation? **What if** we would see healing in our nation in our lifetime?

Gracious Heavenly Father, You are the Ancient of Days, You are the Mighty Judge, and You are the King Eternal. Father, our nation is broken and sick. We acknowledge that the hardships and disasters we face are the consequences of our own waywardness. We confess that we are deserving of Your discipline and punishment. But Lord, we know that You are merciful. We know that You are quick to forgive when we come before You in an attitude of genuine repentance. We need Your healing hand to cover us. Lord, call us to daily confess our own sin and the sin of our nation before You. Place a spirit of repentance within us. Cause us to mourn and grieve over our sin and the affront it has been to You. You alone can heal our land Lord. You alone can remove the offenses. You alone can restore. You alone can give us a future and a hope. In Jesus' Name, Amen.

PERSONAL REFLECTION

1. How do you deal with the issue of sin in your own life? Do you deny it, justify it, or rationalize it? Do you go to God in repentance?

2. What does it mean to you that David's sin was never mentioned again in Scripture? How do you apply that to your own life?

3. Do you think obedience is as important today as it was in biblical times? Why or why not?

4. What relationship do you think exists between our obedience or disobedience, and the things that happen to us or our world? Please explain your answer. Can you cite examples?

5. On a scale of one to ten (one being the least and ten being the greatest) how aware are you that you are the temple of the Holy Spirit and that today God tabernacles within you? What does that mean to you? How does it affect your behavior and choices?

6. Which three **what ifs** spoke to you the most?

7
ON A WALL WITH A PRAYER
II Kings 18-19; II Chronicles 32

The nation of Israel reached its pinnacle under the leadership of King David and his son, Solomon. God showered Solomon with much favor and riches. He ruled the people in wisdom and justice. Solomon fulfilled God's promise to David and built the house for God that his father had desired and designed. But Solomon did not end his reign or his life well. His love for many women (three hundred wives and seven hundred concubines)[50] replaced his love for God and they led his heart astray. There is much to be said for beginning well; even more important is the act of ending well. Following his death, it did not take long before Israel began its descent into spiritual decay.

Solomon's son, Rehoboam, neither began nor ended well. Under his leadership the nation of Israel divided into two kingdoms – the Northern, sometimes referred to as Israel, and the Southern, also known as Judah. Often these two factions were at war with each other. Over the years kings were born and kings died. In the Northern Kingdom sometimes rebellion and mutiny would unseat a king and a new one would ascend the throne. None of the nineteen kings who sat upon the throne of Israel were considered faithful in God's eyes. However, the kingly bloodline of David was always maintained in the Southern Kingdom, Judah. Some of the kings were remembered for "doing what was right in the eyes of the Lord," but most of them were not.

As goes the king, so goes the kingdom. Over the years, both nations ignored the commands of God. Like wayward and rebellious children, they thumbed their noses and ran after other gods, who were not gods at all. How the heart of Father God must have broken as He watched His beloved children not only reject Him, but also the blessings He desired to shower on them. How His heart must have filled with anguish knowing the discipline He would have to administer.

In His longsuffering, God continued to reach out for hundreds of years. Eventually God's hand of protection was removed and the Northern Kingdom, Israel, fell to the Assyrian army. The people were taken captive and the land became desolate:

All this took place because the Israelites had sinned against the Lord their God, who had brought them up out of Egypt from under the power of Pharaoh king of Egypt.[51]

The remainder of II Kings chapter seventeen enumerates a long list of their offenses and sins against God.

One might think that the Southern Kingdom, Judah, would have learned from the downfall of her "sister kingdom." She did not, and although Judah continued to exist for about one hundred fifty more years, she also continued in a spiritual downward spiral.

In 726 BC, King Hezekiah assumed the throne of Judah. He was a ripe old age of twenty five at the time. We might refer to King Hezekiah as "one of the good guys." He was of the bloodline of David and was the twelfth king to ascend the throne of Judah after the split of the two kingdoms. King Hezekiah was like a breath of fresh air amidst a stench; he was like a bright light in darkness.

Hezekiah trusted in the Lord, the God of Israel. There was no one like him among all the kings of Judah, either before him or after him. He held fast to the Lord and did not cease to follow him; he kept the commands the Lord had given Moses. And the Lord was with him; he was successful in whatever he undertook.[52]

Despite this glowing assessment, the situation around Hezekiah was anything but bright. Four years after he became king, the Assyrian army attacked and laid siege to the capital of Northern Israel, Samaria. Two years later, Israel finally fell and her people were taken captive to Assyria.

Eight years after that, the same Assyrian army began its attack against the cities in Judah, and eventually her capital, Jerusalem.

The Assyrian army had a reputation for being particularly skilled and intensely brutal in warfare. According to historian Simon Anglim:

The Assyrians created the world's first great army and the world's first great empire. This was held together by two factors: their superior abilities in siege warfare and their reliance on sheer, unadulterated terror. It was Assyrian policy always to demand that examples be made of those who resisted them; this included deportations of entire peoples and horrific physical punishments. One inscription from a temple in the city of Nimrod records the fate of the leaders of the city of Suru on the Euphrates River, who rebelled from, and were reconquered by, King Ashurbanipal:

"I built a pillar at the city gate and I flayed all the chief men who had revolted and I covered the pillar with their skins; some I walled up inside the pillar, some I impaled upon the pillar on stakes."

Such punishments were not uncommon. Furthermore, inscriptions recording these vicious acts of retribution were displayed throughout the empire to serve as a warning.[53]

Words such *as massacred, razed, felled by the sword, impaled on poles and barbaric* are frequently used in describing the acts of this army. Their tactics were designed to intentionally instill fear into those they were attacking. Their reputation preceded them. The term terrorists might easily be applied to them. In fact, the Assyrian army might well be the forerunners of the terrorists in the world today.

This was the army with which Hezekiah had to contend.

They were extremely skilled in implementing psychological warfare. Outside city walls they would shout terrifying threats so the people inside could hear and be paralyzed with fear.

On at least one occasion they did this very thing. II Kings 18:19-25 says:

The field commander said to them, "Tell Hezekiah:

" 'This is what the great king, the king of Assyria, says: On what are you basing this confidence of yours? You say you have strategy and military strength – but you speak only empty words. On whom are you depending, that you rebel against me? Look now, you are depending on Egypt, that splintered reed of a staff, which pierces a man's hand and wounds him if he leans on it! Such is Pharaoh king of Egypt to all who depend on him. And if you say to me, "We are depending on the Lord our God" – isn't he the one whose high places and altars Hezekiah removed, saying to Judah and Jerusalem, "You must worship before the altar in Jerusalem"?

"Come now, make a bargain with my master, the king of Assyria: I will give you two thousand horses – if you can put riders on them! How can you repulse one officer of the least of

my master's officials, even though you are depending on Egypt for chariots and horsemen? Furthermore, have I come to attack and destroy this place without word from the Lord? The Lord himself told me to march against this country and destroy it.'"

Did you catch the fear tactics? Did you catch the mockery? Did you catch the sarcasm and cynicism? Did you catch the disdain? Did you catch the ridicule? Did you catch the deception? Picture this powerful, formidable, and barbaric army right outside the city gates, boasting of their past conquests, and shouting threats intended to terrorize.

He goes on to chide:

"Do not listen to Hezekiah, for he is misleading you when he says, 'The Lord will deliver us.' Has the god of any nation ever delivered his land from the hand of the King of Assyria?"[54]

Anglim gives us some insight into what the people inside the wall may not only have heard, but saw:

The city was first surrounded to prevent escape. Next, archers were brought forward; under the cover of giant shields, they cleared the battlements. The king then used the tried-and-tested Assyrian method of building an earthen ramp close to the enemy wall, covering it with flat stone and wheeling forward a machine that combined a siege-tower with a battering ram. The Assyrians then staged a two-pronged assault. The tower was wheeled up the ramp and the ram was brought to bear against the mid-section of the enemy wall. Archers in the tower cleared the battlements while bowmen on the ground pushed up close to the wall to cover an infantry assault with scaling ladders. The fighting appears to have been intense, and the assault probably took several days, yet eventually the Assyrians entered the city. Archaeology has revealed that the place was looted and hundreds of men, women, and children were put to the sword. The relief of the siege [at Nineveh] shows prisoners begging for mercy at the feet of Sennacherib. Others less fortunate, perhaps the leaders were impaled on stakes.[55]

Terror must have gripped the hearts of the people, as the horror of their fate seemed inescapable.

What was Hezekiah, a man who was virtually unskilled in this kind of warfare, to do? He seemed to be between a rock and a hard place.

This is what he did not do. He did not respond to the threats. He did not engage himself in conversation with the commander of the army. He did not try to compromise. He did not pick up a weapon. He did not try to rally his army for physical warfare. He did not go and hide. He did not surrender. He did not shake his fist and curse God.

He did the only thing he knew to do. He turned to the only warfare he knew. He turned to the only Warrior he knew – the Warrior who is mightier than any other warrior.

What he did appeared to be a senseless, ridiculous response. In actuality, it was the most powerful form of warfare. He tore his clothes, put on sackcloth, went to the temple, sought the Word of the Lord from the prophet, and prayed and prayed and prayed and prayed. His prayer is recorded in II Kings 19:15-19:

"O LORD, God of Israel, enthroned between the cherubim, you alone are God over all the kingdoms of the earth. You have made heaven and earth. Give ear, O LORD, and hear; open your eyes, O LORD, and see; listen to the word Sennacherib has sent to insult the living God.

"It is true, O Lord, that the Assyrian kings have laid waste these nations and their lands. They have thrown their gods into

the fire and destroyed them, for they were not gods but only wood and stone, fashioned by men's hands. Now, O LORD our God, deliver us from his hand, so that all kingdoms on earth may know that you alone, O LORD, are God."

And don't you know, God answered? Without ever having to pick up a physical weapon, God rousted the Assyrian army that day by creating a circumstance which resulted in their leaving. They never threw a spear; they never built a ramp; they never put ladders against the wall; they never captured or killed a single Israelite, and they never fulfilled any of their threats. One intervention from God in response to prayer and – boom! – the enemy was sent running!

This is a story with a good ending, but it could have ended so differently. **What if** Hezekiah had responded differently? **What if** he had cowered and succumbed to the demands of the Assyrians? **What if** he had given in to the psychological manipulation of the threats? **What if** he had believed their words? **What if** he had tried to placate them? **What if** he had chosen denial, pretending everything was alright? **What if** he had shouted at God, "After all I have done to worship you, you allow this to happen?"

There is no question that Hezekiah and Judah were in a crisis situation. **What if** Hezekiah had not spent a lifetime developing a relationship with the Lord, so that in the time of trouble he had nowhere to turn? **What if** he had not known and trusted in the character and faithfulness of his God? **What if** Hezekiah had turned to idol gods to help him, as some other kings had?

Or **what if** Hezekiah had leaned on his own understanding and his own abilities? **What if** he had depended on Egypt to come to his rescue, as the Assyrian commander had accused? **What if** he had turned to the counsel of man to direct his response?

What if Hezekiah had responded to the words and threats in anger? **What if,** out of pride, he had challenged the enemy army? **What if** he had mustered the fledgling troops that he had and sent them out to battle? **What if** he had taken things into his own hands in any of these or other ways?

The story would have ended very differently - and very tragically.

In our own lives, we may not be facing the Assyrian army, but we all experience crises on some level. We may not be on a visual and literal battlefield, but we all contend with a formidable foe. That enemy is out to destroy us. His tactics may be subtle, or they may be very overt. He threatens, chides, shames, lies, deceives, manipulates, torments, accuses, blames, oppresses, frightens, cripples, paralyzes, demoralizes, and terrorizes. He will stop at nothing to achieve his purposes. His goal is to steal, kill, and destroy those who are made in the image of God. He does not take a vacation, sleep, take a coffee break, or punch out on the time clock. No one is off his radar screen. He whispers lies into our ears and plants seeds of torment in our thoughts. He is the same one who instigated the fall of Adam and Eve in the Garden of Eden, and he has not stopped since. His name is Satan, Lucifer, the deceiver, the accuser of the brethren.

Our battle with him may not be visible to the physical eye, but it is real, and it is gruesome. It may not be audible to the physical ear, but it is real, and it can be devastating. No one is exempt. No one gets a pass. And his goal for each one of us is utter destruction. He is serious, and if we are going to defeat him, we need to be serious also.

What if we responded to our enemy the same way King Hezekiah responded to the Assyrians? **What if** we did not engage in conversation with our enemy? In II Kings 18:36, King Hezekiah's instruction to the people was to not answer the Assyrian commander, and therefore they were silent. Engaging in conversation with the enemy only gives him an invitation to talk more.

What if we did not let his words ring in our ears? **What if** we did not succumb to his deceit? **What if** we did not allow tape recordings of his lies to play over and over again in our minds? **What if** we spent time in God's Word so that we knew real truth and could readily identify our enemy's deceptive tactics? **What if** our relationship with our Heavenly Father was such that in times of attack, we ran to Him as our strong tower and our refuge? **What if** we hid ourselves in Him and let Him send the enemy running? **What if** instead of turning to others to complain, we would turn to them for prayer in times of trouble? **What if** we would humble ourselves before God, pray, and trust Him to fight our battles as He said He would?

The outcome of our battles might be amazingly different.

Bullying is a hot topic in our society today. According to the American Psychological Association, bullying is a form of aggressive behavior in which someone intentionally and repeatedly causes another person injury or discomfort. Bullying can take the form of physical contact, words, or more subtle action. The bullied individual typically has trouble defending him or herself and does nothing to "cause" the bullying.[56]

The old saying "sticks and stones may break my bones, but words will never hurt me" is a lie in itself. Broken bones are visible, but they heal. Emotional wounds caused by unkind words pierce deeply and cannot be seen, but they take a long time to heal, and sometimes never do. How many times in recent years have we heard of a young person harming themselves or even taking their life because of this practice of bullying? Just as the commander of the Assyrian army used words to psychologically damage the people of Judah, the words we speak to one another can have the same effect.

Who has not been the recipient of words that deeply stung at some point in their lives? Even if the language or the intent is not as severe as the American Psychological Association's definition of bullying, words matter, and words can hurt. The book of Proverbs addresses the matter of the tongue. Perhaps one of the most concise and convicting statements is found in Proverbs 18:21.

The tongue has the power of life and death, and those who love it will eat its fruit.

What if we learned from this that we do not want to be the ones that allow such harmful words to come from our mouths? **What if** we practiced Psalm 141:3?

Set a guard over my mouth, O Lord; keep watch over the door of my lips.

What if we purposed in our heart to follow Psalm 19:14?

May the words of my mouth and the meditation of my heart be pleasing in your sight, O Lord, My Rock and my Redeemer.

What if we learned how to combat in a godly way the destructive words that might be spoken to or over us? **What if** instead of taking things into our own hands, we allow God to be our protector? **What if** we didn't retaliate, but let God be our vindicator? **What if** we knew who we were in Christ so well that the effects of lies, accusation, blaming, shaming, criticizing, shunning, and negativity just rolled off our backs? **What if** we knew who we were in Christ so well that the words found no place to take root within us? **What if** we learned to take these verbal attacks to the Lord in prayer, as Hezekiah did? **What if** we applied the principle of forgiveness to those who might speak wrongly so that the power of their words were broken? **What if** we walked in forgiveness, so that we did not give the enemy a foothold? **What if** we went even beyond forgiveness and did good to those who hate us, blessed those who curse us, and prayed for those who despitefully use us?[57]

Would we not experience freedom, joy, and victory as Hezekiah and his people must have experienced when they looked outside the wall and saw that their enemy was gone? Would we not be relieved of the guilt that follows when we allow ourselves to be caught up in confrontation? Would we not be filled with a sense of satisfaction in knowing we had done what was right in the Lord's eyes? Would we not know the peace that passes understanding which comes from trusting Jesus to fight our battles?

This story applies not only to our personal battles with the enemy, but to our nation today. Terror and terrorism have taken a forefront in our news. Since September 11, 2001, our nation has dealt with both actual and threatened attacks of a heinous and barbaric nature. We are constantly on the alert for impending dangers that we have never known on our soil before. Every aspect of this hideous situation is to instill fear and cripple us. Al Qaeda and ISIS and other terror organizations desire to not only strip us of the life we know, but to annihilate us.

What if we give into that fear? **What if** we let it paralyze us and change our lifestyle, our values, and our principles? **What if** we cower in trepidation? **What if** we allow that terror to incite us to turn on one another instead of the real enemy?

Then we are already defeated, and we are already history.

I am so thankful for the courageous and beyond-brave men and women who put their lives on the line every day to protect our nation and that for which it stands. Their task is ominous and of utmost importance; they are to be honored and admired for their skill and their selflessness.

But as skilled as they may be, as trained as they may be, as strong as they may be, and as well-equipped as they may be, they need the Presence and Power of Almighty God leading them in order to be victorious. Not all of us can be in the physical battle, but we can all take up our arms in the spiritual battle. **What if** we were committed to cover our men and women in uniform with prayer? **What if** all across this nation prayers were lifted to God each day on behalf of our troops? **What if** all across this nation prayers were lifted to God every day on behalf of our police men and women? **What if** we were to admit that even the best military in the world cannot overcome oppression without the intervention of God? **What if** we would genuinely recognize that we cannot depend upon the military in and of itself to fight this battle? **What if** we truly embraced the truth that "'*it is not by might, nor by power, but by my Spirit,' says* the *Lord*"?[58] **What if** we followed the example of King Hezekiah, who in the face of extreme threat and terror, humbled himself and cried out to the Lord in earnest and passionate prayer?

In hardships, crisis, and difficulties of any kind, where do we turn for help? **What if** our immediate response was always to bow our knee and with uplifted hands turn our face to the One Who sits on the Throne of Grace?

Lord Jesus, in the times in which we live, teach us to be strong and of good courage in the face of impending danger. Silence the voice of the enemy in our own lives, and in the life of our nation. Cause us to rebuke his threats, lies, and deception. Teach us how to fight in the spiritual realm with the truth of Your Word. Cause us to run to you in times of need, to cry out to you, and to trust you, as King Hezekiah did. We ask that you put a shield of protection over those in our military and police who everyday make such sacrifices to uphold freedom. Even though we do not deserve it Lord, we ask for your mighty and miraculous intervention in the decisions and battles of our nation. Lord, we acknowledge we are desperate for your forgiveness and mercy in our land. In Jesus' Name, Amen.

PERSONAL REFLECTION

1. What are your thoughts regarding beginning well and ending well? Are you familiar with a situation in which someone began well and did not end well? Have you ever personally been in such a situation? What did you learn?

2. Have you ever been in a situation when someone was intentionally trying to create fear within you? How did you handle that situation? What can you/we learn from Hezekiah's situation?

3. How can we apply Hezekiah's situation to our nation today?

4. What three **what ifs** spoke to you the most? Would you add any?

8
A MAN WITH A VISION
Daniel 9:4-19

Hezekiah's prayers of desperation pounded the gates of Heaven. The open ears of God heard and received them. The gracious hand of God moved and covered the city of Jerusalem with His mighty protection. For at least a time, the Southern Kingdom, Judah, was free from enemy invasion. One would think that having experienced such obvious divine intervention, the people would be forever grateful, obedient, and reverent to such a merciful God. They were not.

Within one generation they returned to their sinful ways. Hezekiah's own son, Manasseh, was the most wicked king to sit upon the throne of Judah. His despicable ways led the nation quickly down a slippery slope towards certain judgment. Interestingly enough, Manasseh himself ended his life well, as he turned to God in repentance in his later years. Amazingly enough, God forgave and restored him despite the horrific acts he had committed. But tragically enough, the nation never recovered and continued to multiply sin upon sin.

At the same time this spiritual, moral, and political decay was mounting up within the kingdom of Judah, there was a shifting of power among the nations outside the kingdom. In 605 BCE, Nineveh, the capital city of Assyria, was attacked.[59] [60] The Assyrian Empire crumbled and was replaced by the Babylonian Empire as the primary "power player" in the region. Although the Babylon army, under the leadership of

Nebuchadnezzar, was not as ruthless as the Assyrians, conquest of neighboring lands was still the primary objective.[61]

Babylon picked up where Assyria left off, and Judah found herself in the grip of a new enemy. It did not take long before the people of Judah once again found themselves under siege. This siege initially took the form of demanding tribute. When resistance to paying that tribute arose, food and water supplies were cut off and inhabitants were taken captive.

Sources vary slightly as to the exact dates that captives were taken, but they do agree that somewhere between 605 BCE and 581 BCE there were three separate waves of deportation.[62] This deportation was known as the Diaspora. Fortunately for those taken captive, Babylon's treatment of exiles was much different from what the Assyrian treatment had been.

For the most part the exiles were not treated as prisoners or criminals. Although King Nebuchadnezzar is best known in history for his military conquests and power, Jewish tradition views him in a predominantly favorable and positive light.[63] King Nebuchadnezzar allowed most of the exiles to settle in towns and villages and create their own communities in Babylon. They were allowed to farm or participate in any livelihood they could find. Many became comfortable in this new location. Some of them even became wealthy in their new society. One might surmise this was a blessing for the exiles. In reality it contributed to their detriment as they became so comfortable they lost their desire to return to Jerusalem. They also considered themselves to be better off than those who had been left behind in desolate Judah. Instead of their hearts longing for the God of Israel, many became cold and hardened towards Him.[64]

Among those taken captive during the initial exile, somewhere around 600 BCE, were four young men: Daniel, Hananiah, Mischael, and Azariah. We know that these were outstanding young men, because King Nebuchadnezzar had stipulated that only those who were without physical defect, handsome, having an aptitude for learning, well-informed, quick to learn, and qualified for serving were to be brought into the palace in Babylon.[65]

Daniel, Hananiah, Mishael, and Azariah were not average exiles. There is a possibility that they may have been royalty, but not of the kingly bloodline. They may have spent their early years in the palace in Jerusalem.[66] King Nebuchadnezzar, or at least his officials, spied unique and desirable qualities in these four young men. It was determined they were worthy of special training for the king's court.

King Nebuchadnezzar's empire was rapidly expanding at this point and he needed capable, intelligent young men to help rule his kingdom. He was intentional and specific in identifying those who could step into positions of leadership that might be available. These four definitely met the job description.

Even though this might sound like a great compliment, even though palace living might sound desirable, this was no "cake walk" for these adolescents. Imagine what it must have been like for them to be taken from everything that was familiar to them: their families, the temple, their homes, their friends, their foods, and their lifestyle in general. Imagine what the several hundred mile journey, probably on foot, to a foreign land must have been like. Think of what it must have been like to have suddenly been thrown into a totally different culture through no choice of your own, and with no preparation. Think of what it must have been like to wonder if you would ever lay your eyes on lost loved ones and loved places again.

This was not an easy thing for any fifteen to eighteen year old to endure.

Shortly after their arrival in Babylon, the indoctrination process began. The intention was to first remove all remnants of their physical, emotional, mental, and especially spiritual connection with their Jewish background. The second purpose was to immerse them into the Babylonian way of life. The point was to assimilate them into Babylonian culture by changing their identity, their allegiance, their calling, their faith, and their very personhood.

The first thing that probably happened to these handsome, physically fit and healthy young boys was that they were made eunuchs. There is some disagreement as to what this actually meant. The word used in the original text is *"saris,"* and it can either mean to "emasculate" or "chief official." Although we know these young men did become officials in the court, there is a higher probability of the word meaning emasculate in this context. Cross referencing it with words of warning from the prophets Isaiah and Jeremiah, we find this same word used as a form of judgment during captivity. This was a practice typically done when virile young men were brought into the king's court to prevent them from being sexually tempted. It was sometimes used to inflict humiliation and cause demoralization. It is doubtful this was the intent with Daniel and his friends. More likely it was for the purpose of ensuring loyalty and allegiance.[67]

That's a lot for any fifteen to eighteen year old young man to endure.

The second thing the Babylonians did was to change their names. In Hebrew cultures, names are very significant and often identified a person's character or relationship to God. In Hebrew, Daniel's name meant "God is my Judge." His name was changed to Belteshazzar, which meant "Bel (a god of the Babylonians) protect his life". Hananiah meant "the Lord shows grace," he was given the name Shadrach which meant "under the command of Aku," the moon god. Mishael meant "who is like God?" but his new name, Meshach meant "who is like Aku?" Finally, Azariah meant "the Lord helps," but his Babylonian name, Abednego, meant "servant of Nebo."[68] All of this was done to eradicate their memories of Judah and especially the God and Judah, and be assimilated into Babylonian culture and thought.

That's a lot for any fifteen to eighteen year old to endure. Many others would have caved to the pressure. Many others did cave to the pressure and the process. But not these four.

Scripture says in Daniel 1:8:

But Daniel resolved not to defile himself with...

This was not a casual decision. Resolve implies determination, dedication, tenacity, and steadfastness. It was not a temporary decision, but one that would influence every choice and every action that Daniel would make for the rest of his life. Although it doesn't specify, I think history would confirm that his three friends made the same resolution. Such a resolution is, to say the least, pretty gutsy of four adolescent boys. And yet it seems that making this decision at the very beginning of their introduction to Babylonian life served them well throughout their stay. They adhered to it regardless of demands, threats, danger, ridicule, mockery, and isolation. Many times their faith in the God of Israel was challenged. Many times it was put on trial. Many times that faith was tested to the extent of fiery flames, lion dens, and other threats of death. Each time these four stood unwavering, knowing that their God was able to deliver them. And each time He did.

We don't know what happened to Daniel's three friends after their encounter when the Lion of Judah closed the mouths of the lions of King Darius. We do know God delivered them, unscathed, without a scratch. The Bible does not mention them after that incident.

We do know, however, that Daniel lived a very long life – at least into his upper eighties. During those sixty plus years as a captive in Babylon he was confronted daily with the pagan life of those around him. During those sixty plus years he was given opportunity after opportunity to compromise his beliefs. During those sixty plus years there were incidents upon incidents when he endured criticism for his faith. But Daniel remained faithful and steadfast in his convictions. His enemies once said of him:

"We will never find any basis for charges against this man Daniel unless it has something to do with the law of his God."[69]

Oh Lord, may that be said of each one of us!

Daniel remained true to his resolve to not defile himself with the practices of Babylon. He remained true to praying to his God three times every day.[70] He remained true to reading whatever Scripture he could get his hands on.[71] Because of this resolve, God's favor was showered upon Daniel and he rose to respected positions within several of the kings' courts. Officials on every level of government sought Daniel for his counsel and guidance. They honored him for his wisdom.

It speaks volumes that a man who had lived among a godless and hostile people for sixty plus years still adhered to the God of Israel. Many others would have assimilated to the culture around them, rationalizing and justifying that it just wasn't worth the cost to stay pure. It is precious that we find Daniel, during the later years of his life, still reading the Scriptures and seeking God and His truth. With blurry and dimmed vision, Daniel tenderly held in his knobby hands the Word of the Lord.

That is where we find him in Daniel chapter nine. As he is reading the word of the prophet Jeremiah, he has a revelation. Jeremiah was a contemporary of Daniel, although probably decades older. When Daniel was taken as a youth, Jeremiah was left in Jerusalem, speaking God's Word of warning to the people. They may or may not have known each other, but I imagine at one time or another their paths crossed. Maybe as a child Daniel had even heard the prophet speak. I imagine the prophecies of Jeremiah were particularly precious to Daniel. Perhaps he had even carried them on parchments of paper with him during the exile.

In two passages[72] the prophet declares that God promised to bring His people back to Jerusalem at the end of seventy years' captivity in Babylon. Imagine Daniel reading the promise; imagine the wheels in his brain turning as he calculates the time period. He has been in Babylon more than sixty years! This Word takes on new life for him. It fills him with new hope! The end is in sight! Imagine the joy and anticipation that must have filled him! Imagine him jumping up, pulling up his tunic so as not to trip as he runs around shouting, "We're going home!"

Yet even greater than that joy, Daniel was overwhelmed with a spirit of devotion, of worship, and of adoration. He was compelled to fast, put on sackcloth and ashes, and fall prostrate before His God in deep repentance, earnest supplication, and utmost reverence. And this magnificent prayer came from his lips:

"O Lord, the great and awesome God, who keeps his covenant of love with all who love him and obey his commands, we have sinned and done wrong. We have been wicked and have rebelled; we have turned away from your command and laws. We have not listened to your servants the prophets, who spoke in your name to our kings, our princes and our fathers, and to all the people of the land.

"LORD, you are righteous, but this day we are covered with shame – the men of Judah and people of Jerusalem and all Israel, both near and far, in all the countries where you have scattered us because of our unfaithfulness to you. O LORD, we and our kings, our princes and our fathers are covered with shame because we have sinned against you. The Lord our God is merciful and forgiving, even though we have rebelled against him; we have not obeyed the Lord our God or kept the laws he gave us through his servants the prophets. All Israel has transgressed your law and turned away, refusing to obey you.

"Therefore the curses and sworn judgments written in the Law of Moses, the servant of God, have been poured out on us, because we have sinned against you. You have fulfilled the words spoken against us and against our rulers by bringing upon us this disaster. Under the whole heaven nothing has ever been done like what has been done to Jerusalem. Just as it is written in the Law of Moses, all this disaster has come upon us, yet we have not sought the favor of the LORD our God by turning from our sins and giving attention to your truth. The LORD did not hesitate to bring the disaster upon us, for the LORD our God is righteous in everything he does; yet we have not obeyed him.

"Now, O Lord our God, who brought your people out of Egypt with a mighty hand and who made for yourself a name that endures to this day, we have sinned, we have done wrong. O Lord, in keeping with all your righteous acts, turn away your anger and your wrath from Jerusalem, your city, your holy hill. Our sins and the iniquities of our fathers have made Jerusalem and your people an object of scorn to all those around us.

"Now, our God, hear the prayers and petitions of your servant. For your sake, O Lord, look with favor on your desolate sanctuary. Give ear, O God, and hear; open your eyes and see the desolation of the city that bears your Name. We do not make requests of you because we are righteous, but because of your great mercy. O Lord, listen! O Lord, forgive! O Lord, hear and act! For your sake, O my God, do not delay, because your city and your people bear your Name."[73]

It is significant to note that while Daniel must have experienced exhilaration at the prospect of his people returning home, he, himself, would never see Jerusalem again. His name is not mentioned in the records found in Ezra or Nehemiah as one of the exiles who returned to the homeland. At almost ninety years of age, it is doubtful that Daniel would be able to make the five hundred mile journey he made as a youth.

And yet the prospect of the promise given by the prophet Jeremiah being fulfilled thrilled his soul. It is also significant to note that while the prophecy spoke of future events, Daniel's prayer was focused on the past. While it is true that in earlier passages he had been seeking understanding of future events, at this point he turned his concerns to Israel's long and sordid history. Nowhere in his prayer do we find Daniel asking God to fulfill the prophecy. Instead, he concentrated on the sins of the people that resulted in them being taken to Babylon in the first place.

He proclaimed the goodness and righteousness of God throughout the prayer. He enumerated and confessed the sins of his fellow Israelites. He admitted they solely shouldered the blame and that God was just for meting out his discipline. He implored God, not for his own sake, and not for the sake of the people, but for the sake of Jerusalem, the sanctuary, and for God's Holy Name.

Daniel apparently understood something that we often overlook. It is virtually impossible for the future to be healthy and blessed if the past is strewn with unresolved garbage. So often we want to just sweep our failures, mistakes and sins under the carpet, and go with the old adage, "out of sight, out of mind". In doing so we simply drag the rubbish with us.

Daniel understood the appalling offense Israel's mounting sin was to God. He realized that even though they had fulfilled their "sentence," unless they acknowledged their sin and sought God for forgiveness they would just go back to their same old disobedient patterns.

In this moment Daniel was standing at a crossroads. He was in the present, looking forward to the future, yet very much aware that the past was impacting both. One sentence in his prayer, *"...yet we have not sought the favor of the Lord our God by turning from our sins and giving attention to your truth,"[74]* indicates that despite all the Israelites had been through, they had not yet turned their hearts and their loyalty back to God. Their increasing waywardness and idolatry had been what had gotten them into this predicament in the first place. That predicament was extreme, yet they still had not learned the lesson, even after seventy years.

I imagine that realization gripped Daniel's heart. Here they were, very near the end of their captivity, on the threshold of freedom to return home, and their hearts were still far, if not farther, from God. I imagine his prayer was birthed from a recognition of that fact. I imagine he must have pondered and grieved their spiritual condition. To what avail had the people endured this chastisement? Had their hardened hearts been softened, or were they just as steeped in sin? Had their hearts been taken more captive than their bodies were? Would they choose to stay in Babylon, enjoying the opulent life, and not return to Jerusalem when they were set free? Were they so blinded by what was empty that they could no longer cling to the promises of God? Were their ears deaf to His beckoning? Would they choose the gods of Babylon over the God of Israel? If they did return to Jerusalem, would they just pick up where they left off? Had they learned anything? Had they allowed that learning to transform them?

Daniel was driven to his knees in prayer. As God's prophet to the people he "stood in the gap"[75] to intercede. He was paving the way for their return, as repentance is always the first step in our relationship with God. In essence, he took upon himself the responsibility of all the people's sin from the time of Moses, entreating God for mercy and forgiveness, so that they might have a fresh start. Speaking for God, one of the psalmists said:

"He who sacrifices thank offerings honors me, and he prepares the way so that I may show him the salvation of God."[76]

This was precisely what Daniel did. Daniel's prayer of worship and repentance must have pleased the heart of God. While Daniel was still *"speaking and praying, confessing my sin and the sin of my people Israel and making my request to the Lord my God for his holy hill,"*[77] his prayer was interrupted. Perhaps this is the only time Scripture records a prayer being interrupted by another being. The angel Gabriel was sent to deliver a message to Daniel. The message was not in regard to what Daniel was praying, but more in response to it. The motive and earnestness of Daniel's heart blessed God. The burden he felt for his people blessed the heart of God. God's heart always responds to those who come before Him with selfless abandon.

Gabriel was sent to give Daniel insight and understanding of things to come. His brief message is perhaps the most confusing yet specifically prophetic passage in Scripture. It is also verifiable as some of the events predicted have already come to pass in the exact timing Daniel indicated. These three verses found in Daniel 9:24-27 are also the most time-encompassing prophecy in Scripture; for they cover the span of the ages from the end of the captivity to the time of the Tribulation.[78]

Powerful and mind-boggling revelations! Because of Daniel's character, faith and steadfastness, he received and recorded some of most prophetic words from God to mankind. Amos 3:7 says, *"Surely the Sovereign Lord does nothing without revealing his plan to his servants the prophets."*

What if Daniel had not been a man of such character, faith, and steadfastness? **What if** he had not had a maturity way beyond his years, to resolve in the very beginning not to defile himself? How easy it would have been to have given into the indoctrination of Babylon. How easy it would have been to have assimilated into its opulent and idolatrous lifestyle. How tempting it would have been to just go along with the program. **What if** he had done any of those things?

We may not live as exiles in a foreign land, but we are daily confronted with suggestions and temptations that could compromise our walk with the Lord. In today's world there are numerous ways we are constantly bombarded– television, the many facets of the internet, billboards, advertisements, magazines, radio, and peer pressure are just a few examples. **What if** we, as believers, knew our identity in Christ as well as Daniel knew his identity? **What if** we were as confident in that identity as Daniel was of his? **What if** we were so assured of our identity that nothing or no one could mold us into something other than who the Word of God says we are?

    What if we truly believed we are:
- a child of God (John 1:12)
- a friend of Christ (John 15:15)
- chosen and appointed by Christ to bear His fruit (John 15:16)
- justified, completely forgiven and made righteous (Romans 5:1)
- dead to the power of sin's rule in our lives (Romans 6:1-6)
- forever free from condemnation (Romans 8:1)
- a joint heir with Christ and share His inheritance (Romans 8:17)
- given the mind of Christ (I Corinthians 2:16)
- the temple of the Holy Spirit (I Corinthians 3:16; 6:19)
- bought with a price; belong to Christ (I Corinthians 6:19)
- a new creation in Christ (II Corinthians 5:17)
- established, anointed, and sealed by God (II Corinthians 1:21)
- a saint (Ephesians 1:1)
- blessed with every spiritual blessing in Heaven (Ephesians 1: 1)
- adopted as sons in Christ (Ephesians 1:4)
- holy and blameless in His sight (Ephesians 1:4)
- raised with Christ and seated in Heavenly places (Ephesians 2:6)
- in direct access to God through the Holy Spirit (Ephesians 2:18)
- God's workmanship, created in Christ to do good works (Ephesians 2:10)
- made complete in Christ (Colossians 2:10)
- chosen of God, holy and dearly loved (Colossians 3:12)
- sons/daughters of light and not of darkness (I Thessalonians 5:5)
- a chosen generation, royal priesthood, holy nation (I Peter 2:9)

- are given precious promises by God (II Peter 1:4)

-and so many other truths that seal our identity? **What if** we not only believed these truths, but lived our lives in a manner that reflected them? **What if** we embraced them so powerfully that no external force could derail us? **What if** we professed and confessed them to ourselves and to those around us so that there was no question as to who and Whose we are? **What if** we reminded ourselves and each other of our true identity every day? Would we not grow in the absolute assurance and confidence that who we are is sealed in Christ alone?

Because Daniel knew not only who he was, but more importantly to Whom he belonged, he was able to quickly resolve he would not defile himself. **What if** our resolve was not to be defiled by the world? **What if** we encouraged one another in that resolve as Daniel and his friends did? **What if** we developed a strategy to maintain that resolve? **What if** our spirits were sensitive to the enemy's tactics of weakening our resolve? **What if** we trusted God in every situation where that resolve might be challenged? **What if** we were not afraid of the cost of honoring that commitment?

Living in the midst of massive ungodliness for many decades, Daniel was able to uphold his resolve because of his ongoing devotion to and relationship with his God. Through prayer he kept the doors of communication open. A life of prayer had taught him how to reach Heaven and the heart of God. Reading the Scriptures revealed to him the ways and will of God, gave him insight into the waywardness of man, and allowed him understanding of the times. In the midst of a desert, he found living water. In the midst of captivity, he found true freedom.

In the midst of despair he found hope. In the midst of living as a slave in the court of an earthly king, he found he was really a prince who could have a relationship with the

King of Kings. Even though he had been emasculated, he found life-giving purpose through his relationship with his Maker.

Can there ever be enough prayer? Can there ever be too much feasting on the Word of God? **What if** we had the practice of praying and reading Scripture as Daniel did? **What if** we sought the Lord's guidance for every step and every decision we made? **What if** we recognized that all wisdom comes from Him? **What if** in every situation we would turn to Him to instruct our paths? **What if** we realized what an incredible gift prayer is, allowing us to speak with the Almighty? **What if** we took the time to wait upon Him and listen for His answer? **What if** we truly believed that through prayer God reveals His plans, purposes, and secrets to us? **What if** we truly recognized and embraced the power that prayer unleashes? **What if** we believed that through prayer we have the ability to change things?

What if we delighted in reading God's Word? **What if** we read it from a heart of devotion instead of a heart of obligation? **What if** we allowed His Word to permeate our deepest being? **What if** we invited the Word to invade us and transform us? **What if** we allowed His Truth to saturate our thinking? **What if** we walked a path that was lit by His Word?[79] **What if** we too, as Daniel, searched the Scriptures for understanding of the future? God knows all things and His plans and purposes will come to pass. He desires to share his intentions with those who diligently seek Him.

It was through reading the Scripture that Daniel came to the realization of why he and his people had been taken captive. It was through reading the Scripture that he became aware of the extent of his people's perpetual offensive actions towards God. It was through reading the Scripture that Daniel understood that the situation did not have to be what it was, but that his people had created their own demise. Yet his response was not one of anger, antagonism, blaming, disgust, resentment, exasperation, rationalization, or justification. It was one of humility, remorse, and repentance.

What if we too carried in our hearts, minds, and spirits such attitudes? **What if** we would, *"act justly, love mercy and walk humbly with our God"?*[80] **What if** we would cease pointing fingers at everyone else's sin? **What if** we would take the log out of our own eye that causes us to see other people's actions so unfairly and so pridefully? **What if** we would stop blaming and judging those around us?

What if we were to awaken to the possibility that some of the crises and disasters that happen in our nation might just be God trying to get our attention? **What if** we would open our spiritual ears and hear Him calling us back to Himself? **What if** we would respond to that call through fasting and prayer as Daniel did? **What if** we would stop blaming God and acknowledge our own waywardness? **What if** we would understand that His desire for us is good and that all His actions towards us are from a heart of immeasurable love? **What if** we would prostrate ourselves before Him in humility and genuinely repent for our own sin and the sins of our nation? **What if** we would confess that He is righteous and just and that we are the ones in the wrong?

Would God not be pleased with such an attitude and such a prayer? He was with Daniel. Would God not receive such prayers? He accepted Daniel's. Would God not respond to such prayers with favor? He did with Daniel.

Father God, we come before You proclaiming that You are, You always have been, and You always will be the One and Only Sovereign God over all creation. You are great and awesome, everlasting in love. You are merciful, righteous, just and true. Your goodness abounds throughout the earth. But Lord, we are sinful and we have strayed from Your commands. We have disobeyed You and followed the wicked desires of our hearts. We have piled sin upon sin. They are too numerous to count. Our sins reach to Heaven and are a stench in your nostrils. We have acted in pride and arrogance. We have defied Your righteous ways. We have allowed idols to steal our hearts and lead us far away from You. In truth we do not deserve Your goodness. But as Daniel prayed Lord, in keeping with Your covenant with us through the blood of Jesus Christ, would You turn away Your anger and wrath from America, a nation that was founded on faith in You? Would You look with favor on this nation once again and send forth Your mercy, grace and forgiveness to not just cover our sin, but to wash us and remove it as far as the east is from the west? Because of Your great mercy, O Lord, listen! O Lord, forgive! O Lord, hear and act! For Your sake, O my God, do not delay, because this nation and Your people bear Your Name. In Jesus' Name, Amen.

PERSONAL REFLECTION

1. How does Satan or the world try to steal our identities? What has been your personal experience with that?

2. On a scale of one to ten (one being the least and ten being the most) how secure are you in your identity in Christ? Choose five statements from the scriptures listed concerning our identity in Christ that mean the most to you. Record them below. Why are they important to you?

3. In what ways do you need to walk in your identity in Christ more than you do?

4. What does it mean to you to have resolve about something? Is there something in your life you believe you have made a firm resolution about?

5. How can Daniel's prayer impact your prayer life?

6. Which three **what ifs** speak the most to you? Would you add any?

9

BURDENED FOR A WALL
Nehemiah 1:1-11

Daniel continued to minister while in exile for the remainder of his life. God continued to speak to him and reveal to him mysteries regarding things to come. Over the seventy plus years he was in exile, the kingdom changed hands from the Babylonians, who were overcome by the Medes, to the Persians, who overcame the Medes. The kings of all these powers recognized the hand of God upon Daniel and honored him.

The prophecy from Jeremiah that had given birth to Daniel's prayer of repentance came to pass, just as God said it would. In 539 BCE Persia rose to power over the empire, and a man named King Cyrus reigned on the throne. The following year, in 538 BCE, he wrote a decree giving the Jewish exiles permission to return to their homeland. Permission was also granted for them to rebuild their city which had been left in ruins, and to rebuild their temple, which had been ravaged.[81]

Who was this King Cyrus? God knew him hundreds of years before he was even born. Using the prophet Isaiah, God had told the nation of Judah that he would use a servant named Cyrus to bring his people home and rebuild the ruins.

Who says of Cyrus, "He is my shepherd" And I will accomplish all that I please; he will say of Jerusalem, "Let it be rebuilt," and of the temple, "let its foundations be laid."[82]

What is truly amazing is that when Isaiah spoke this word, Jerusalem had not yet been ravaged, the temple was still standing, and no captives had been taken. No wonder the people thought Isaiah was crazy. But with time, as is always the case when God foretells something, each of those things did happen exactly as God said.

II Chronicles 36:22-23 records the fulfillment of Isaiah's prophecy:

In the first year of Cyrus, king of Persia, in order to fulfill the word of the LORD spoken by Jeremiah, the LORD moved the heart of Cyrus King of Persia to make a proclamation throughout his realm and to put it in writing;

"This is what Cyrus king of Persia says:

" ' The LORD, the God of heaven, has given me all the kingdoms of the earth and has appointed me to build a temple for him at Jerusalem in Judah. Anyone of his people among you- may the LORD his God be with him, and let him go up.' "

So the people were free to return to the homeland: the land God had promised and given them through Moses, the land of their ancestors, the land of the patriarchs and prophets, the land of the covenant. They were not forced to go. It was entirely a matter of choice.

It might seem unusual for a king of an empire to release people to return to and rebuild their homeland. Actually the Jews were not the only people group that had been taken captive by King Nebuchadnezzar for which Cyrus did this. Although the gesture was gracious, it was not void of a self-serving motive. King Cyrus hoped to "purchase" the loyalty of these people, and believed they would provide a buffer zone around the borders of his empire from foreign enemies.[83]

Amazingly, sadly, and tragically, only a small portion of the Jews living in the Persian Empire packed their belongings and headed home. According to some calculations it may have been as minimal as two percent.[84]

What happened to the rest? King Cyrus had opened up this incredible opportunity for the Jews to return to the land God had promised them. He had not only given them permission to go, he had stipulated that whatever they needed to rebuild their beloved city be given to them. He had returned all the belongings of the temple that had been stolen by the Babylonians. Talk about an opportunity of a lifetime!!

Why only two percent? What was up with the remaining ninety-eight percent?

Actually, they fell into two major groups. As was noted in the previous chapter, many of them enjoyed their new lifestyle. Before the Diaspora, life in Judah had become increasingly hard. The people's continual sin had caused God to withdraw His hand of blessing and protection. Instead, they experienced His discipline. In this new place they found plenty, riches, and comfort. The memories of the past, and the allure of the present made them reluctant to leave the one and return to the other. They surmised it was just too much work and they weren't willing to pay the price, nor to take the chance that the trip would not be worth it.

There was also a faction of the exiles who called themselves the *gola* or the *bene gola,* which meant exiles, or children of the exiles.

"...within the crucible of despair and hopelessness, they forged a new national identity and a new religion. The exile was unexplainable; Hebrew history was built on the promise of Yahweh to protect the Hebrews and use them for his purposes in human history. Their defeat and the loss of the land promised to them by Yahweh seemed to imply that their faith in this promise was misplaced. This crisis, a form of cognitive

dissonance (when your view of reality and reality itself do not match one another), can precipitate the most profound despair or the most profound reworking of a world view. For the Jews in Babylon, it did both. "[85]

So most stayed, but a small portion were passionate for the homeland. As the Diaspora had not happened all at once, neither did the return. In reality, it happened in three waves which spanned almost one hundred years. The first group left shortly after the decree was written, in 538 BCE, under the leadership of a man named Zerubbabel. It is interesting to note that had the Diaspora never happened, Zerubbabel would have probably sat on the throne of Judah, as he was in the kingly bloodline of David.[86] The second group arrived in Jerusalem in 458 BCE under the leadership of the priest Ezra. The final group was led by a man named Nehemiah in 445 BCE.

Like Daniel, Nehemiah was a Jewish exile in a foreign land. Unlike Daniel, he had never seen Jerusalem, Judah, or any of the land God had promised the Israelites. Nehemiah had been born in the land of captivity. Even though he had never set a foot in Jerusalem, this beloved city was in his heart.

Nehemiah was a cup-bearer to the King of Persia, Artaxerxes. That fact in itself gives us some insight into the kind of man Nehemiah was.

"A cup-bearer was an officer of high rank in royal courts whose duty it was to serve the drinks at the royal table. On account of the constant fear of plots and intrigues, a person must be regarded as thoroughly trustworthy to hold the position. He must guard against poison in the king's cup and was sometimes required to swallow some of the wine before serving it. His confidential relations with the king often gave him a position of great influence. The position of the cup-

bearer is greatly valued and given to only a select few throughout history."[87]

Obviously Nehemiah was a man of integrity and was highly esteemed and respected. Although he was exposed to the grandeur of the palace, he had not allowed himself to be compromised by its lavish riches. He had not allowed himself to succumb to its sumptuous comfort. He had not given in to the allure of the lavish life it offered. Jerusalem burned in his heart. He was not one of those who had traded his desire for Jerusalem for the hollowness of life in Persia.

Perhaps as a child he had heard those who had been taken from Jerusalem speak of its glory and splendor. Perhaps he listened as they reminisced about the homeland. Perhaps his parents or some others rehearsed in his ears the beauty of the Jewish temple and the magnificence of Jerusalem. Perhaps their words took root in his spirit and stirred a longing in him for something he had never personally known. Perhaps he had created pictures in his mind of what the homeland was like. Perhaps his heart was seared with yearning at a very young age. Perhaps God Himself had planted the love of Jerusalem in his heart.

We will never know for sure, but what we do know is that as a grown man Nehemiah was consumed with concern for Jerusalem. He was focused and he would not be deterred. Psalm 137:5-6 describes his attitude about Jerusalem:

If I forget you, O Jerusalem, May my right hand forget its skill, May my tongue cling to the roof of my mouth If I do not remember you, If I do not consider Jerusalem my highest joy.

He questioned travelers who had been to Judah about the condition of Jerusalem and learned that the people were in great trouble and living in disgrace. In addition, the city walls remained broken down and its gates burned, despite the fact that the first exiles had returned nearly a hundred years prior.

In biblical times, having a wall around a city was absolutely imperative to the safety and life of the city and its people. Walls were often massive in height, width, and depth. Watchmen would stand upon the top of the wall to guard against unwanted outsiders approaching the city. A city without a wall was unprotected and therefore the people inside would live in constant stress, fear, and anxiety, knowing they had no recourse if an enemy did attack. A city without a wall was considered undesirable and having no value. No wonder the people living in Jerusalem were living in disgrace and reproach. Broken walls resulted in broken lives.

Many others might have considered this report inconsequential. To others it might have been somewhat troubling. But to say that Nehemiah was dismayed over the news would be putting it mildly. This news pierced his spirit. It grieved his heart. It brought deep anguish to his soul. The Scripture says when he heard the report he sat down. I imagine this wasn't just a "let me rest for a moment" sitting down; I imagine this was a sitting down because all the strength had drained out of his body. I imagine this was more the kind of collapsing that occurs when one receives some kind of horrific news.

The Scripture says he wept. I imagine this wasn't some kind of quiet tears "trickling down the face" kind of event. I imagine it was an uncontrollable sobbing that comes from the deepest places within. I imagine it was the kind of weeping that causes one's whole body to quiver and tremble in grief. It brings to mind the picture of another One who wept over the broken condition of Jerusalem some four hundred fifty years later.

The Scripture says Nehemiah fasted and prayed. This wasn't some quick prayer shot up to Heaven. This wasn't some, "Help, Lord!" kind of prayer. Nehemiah heard the news in the month of Kislev.[88] This is the ninth month of the Jewish calendar. It wasn't until the month of Nissan, the first month of the Jewish calendar, that he took any kind of action on it.[89]

What do you suppose he was doing during those four months? What do you suppose was consuming his thoughts? I imagine he was praying like he had never prayed before. I imagine he was driven to his knees and storming heaven. I imagine he prayed until he received an answer from God. Day and night he prayed:

"O LORD, God of Heaven, the great and awesome God, who keeps his covenant of love with those who love him and obey his commands, let your ear be attentive and your eyes open to hear the prayer your servant is praying before you day and night for your servants, the people of Israel. I confess the sins we Israelites, including myself and my father's house, have committed against you. We have acted very wickedly toward you. We have not obeyed the commands, decrees and laws you gave your servant Moses.

"Remember the instruction you gave your servant Moses, saying, 'If you are unfaithful, I will scatter you among the nations, but if you return to me and obey my commands, then even if your exiled people are at the farthest horizon, I will gather them from there and bring them to the place I have chosen as a dwelling for my Name.'

"They are your servants and your people, whom you redeemed by your great strength and your mighty hand. O Lord, let your ear be attentive to the prayer of this your servant and to the prayer of your servants who delight in revering your

Name. Give your servant success today by granting him favor in the presence of this man." [90]

Much like the prayer of Daniel, Nehemiah came before God in an attitude of reverence for who God is; and in repentance because of who man is, and what he had done. Like Daniel, Nehemiah recalled God's covenant and stood upon His promises. He reminded God, as though God needed reminding, that He pledged to bring the exiled people back. He ended his prayer asking God to give him favor in the eyes of the king.

As Nehemiah prayed day and night over the months, I am certain God began revealing His vision, direction, and plans to him. The vision was BIG. The plans were BIG. The task was of mammoth proportions. As skilled as he might have been, as great a leader as he might have been, as influential as he might have been, Nehemiah was fully aware that these plans could not be accomplished without the intervention of God.

But God is always steps ahead of us, and He had been laying the groundwork for Nehemiah's mission long before Nehemiah was aware of it. Being cupbearer to the king might be considered a "set-up" by God, or a "shoe-in" for Nehemiah. This was not the first or only time God raised one of His faithful servants to a position of influence within the courts of worldly kings in order to accomplish His purposes. He had done so with Joseph, Moses, Daniel, and Esther. [91]

In the Jewish month of Nissan, as Nehemiah was serving the king, God opened the door for the mission to begin. The king questioned Nehemiah regarding the somberness of his countenance. This could have ended poorly for Nehemiah because normally a king might have a servant executed for not being cheerful in their presence. However, the King of Kings, not King Artaxerxes, was in control of this encounter.

Nehemiah was able to inform the king of his burden for Jerusalem and Scripture says, "it pleased the king to send him back"[92] to Jerusalem. He did not send him back empty handed, but with letters of permission and materials he would need.

Nehemiah made the eight hundred mile journey from Susa to Jerusalem. Neither the journey nor the task were problem-free, but in every adverse situation Nehemiah immediately turned to God in prayer. He was a man of great strength and character, but he knew that any success he experienced was only because the hand of the God of Heaven was upon him. Within fifty-six days, he with the help of others, had rebuilt the wall of Jerusalem that had been in charred rubble for one hundred fifty years. Quite a massive endeavor for someone who was a cupbearer to a king. Quite a feat of engineering for a cupbearer to a king.

Nehemiah was not a patriarch like Abraham. God had never visited his home nor shared a meal with him. God had never cut covenant with him. Nehemiah was not a deliverer like Moses, whom God used to call down plagues of judgment against Egypt and split the Red Sea in two. Nehemiah was not an anointed warrior and king as David was. He never sat on the throne of Judah as Hezekiah had. Nehemiah was not a prophet like Daniel who could interpret dreams and tell of things to come.

Nehemiah was an "ordinary man." In these few passages of Scripture he holds before us an example of godly behavior in the work place. He went to his job every day and did what was required of him. From a worldly perspective the purpose of his life was to serve someone else.

This, however, did not cause him to grumble, murmur, or complain. He didn't criticize or become resentful. Instead, he did his job exceptionally well. He must have carried out all the tasks given him with excellence, for one did not become cupbearer without first being tested and proven worthy. In every situation, Nehemiah showed himself to be trustworthy, diligent, dedicated, and loyal. His behavior and character were beyond reproach. Nehemiah had obviously earned the king's respect and trust.

He was a living example of Colossians 3:23:

Whatever you do, work at it with all your heart, as working for the Lord, not for men, since you know that you will receive an inheritance from the Lord as a reward. It is Christ Jesus you are serving.

What if he had not been diligent? **What if** he had never demonstrated these qualities to begin with? The answer to that is quite simple: he would have never been given the office of cupbearer. He would have never had access to the ear of the king.

What if he had taken his position lightly? **What if,** once he had obtained the position, he became nonchalant in his behavior? **What if** he began showing up late for work, or somehow mishandled the task given to him? **What if** he had engaged in conversations with other servants who were undermining to the king? **What if** Nehemiah had abused his position and exposed things that were to remain in strictest confidence? **What if** he had bred discontent among the other servants? **What if** his loyalty to the king had been compromised?

The answer to those questions is quite simple also: he would have been beheaded.

Yet somehow I believe it was the character of the man, and not the threat of beheading, that caused Nehemiah to walk in such integrity and purity of heart.

What if the same could be said of us? **What if** we demonstrated these qualities in the work place, in our ministries, or in other positions we hold? **What if** we committed to conducting ourselves in an exemplary manner? **What if** it could be said of us that we were people of integrity in all situations? **What if** we had a reputation for being honest and trustworthy? **What if** we would find enjoyment and pleasure in serving others? **What if** our intentions were to help another person achieve their goals? **What if** we were willing to sacrifice ourselves so that another person might succeed? **What if** we were intentional in maintaining confidentiality where necessary?

What if we would cease the grumbling and complaining about trivial things that bother us? **What if** we didn't allow resentment fill our hearts? **What if** we didn't compare ourselves to those around us and feel like we are getting the short end of the stick? **What if** we didn't view the tasks we were given as menial or beneath us? **What if** we purposed to maintain an attitude of loyalty to those around us, instead of edifying ourselves?

Perhaps we would find that we are promoted or entrusted with greater things. Perhaps we would find that our sphere of influence is enlarged. Perhaps we would discover that what we say is received with respect and that our credibility carries weight. Perhaps we would be positioned to do greater things for the Kingdom.

Jesus said, *"Whoever can be trusted with very little can also be trusted with much..."*[93]

Lord, may each of us be found to be good, faithful, and trustworthy servants.

Nehemiah bears proof that it is possible to be loyal to both your job, and the call of God. Yet as loyal as Nehemiah was to King Artaxerxes, his deepest devotion lay somewhere else. As excellently as he served the king, his spirit was bound to his

God, and to the things important to his God. The Scripture could not be more clear that God's heart is for Jerusalem. God has set His hand, His eye, His seal, and His Spirit upon Jerusalem. The passages that reveal His love for this city are numerous. Nehemiah's concern and passion for the well-being of Jerusalem was conceived out of his relationship with his God. Nehemiah's heart was broken with what broke the heart of God. It drove him to his knees, and it drove him to action.

What if we truly sought to know what was in the heart of God? **What if** we strove to know what was important to Him? **What if** we approached His Word with the desire to hear the cry of his heart? **What if** we went before Him in prayer, not to tell Him our needs (which He already knows), but to listen as He shares His? **What if** we allowed His priorities to be our priorities? **What if** we allowed Him to break our heart with the things that break His? **What if** we wept, mourned, fasted and prayed over those things as Nehemiah did? **What if** we availed ourselves to do whatever God led us to do in addressing those things, just as Nehemiah did? **What if** we actually put actions to our words?

There are many things that are important to God: marriage, service, obedience, truth, how we treat one another, faithfulness, righteousness, holiness. The list could go on and on. However, I do not think there is anything of greater importance to Him than the salvation of souls. Our Heavenly Father sent His Son not only to show His love for us, but to provide the way of salvation. Jesus, the Son, came to open the doorway of salvation to every soul. He willingly left His throne in Heaven, where He was worshiped and adored, and came to live among us where He was mocked, ridiculed, spat upon, unjustly accused, beaten, and nailed to a cross. Why would anyone do that? Who does that kind of thing?

Someone Who loves deeply, immensely, passionately, extravagantly, unconditionally, immeasurably, profusely, and relentlessly. Someone Who knew there was no other way, *no other way,* for those He loved to be saved. It was for the salvation of souls that Jesus gave His life. That sole action tells us how important each and every soul is to God. It was an extraordinary, extravagant, lavish and scandalous price to pay, but to God the return was more than worth it.

For God so loved the world that he gave his one and only Son, that whoever believes in him shall not perish but have eternal life. [94]

What if we were to embrace in our lives what is most important to God? **What if** we were to make the winning of souls for the Kingdom our top priority? **What if** we were to make it an even greater priority than it has been? **What if** we guarded our own personal lives from being distracted by so many things of lesser importance? **What if** we would give even as much attention, thought, and energy to the condition of souls as we do to the clothes in our closets, the degrees behind our names, the balance in our checking accounts, the size of our homes, the impression we are making on others? These things will all pass away, but the state of one's soul is eternal.

What if the Church reflected the heart of God for the lost? Please don't get me wrong here. I love the Church, but I must ask the question: has the Church in America strayed in any way from her primary mission? Has she become a type of social club? Has she become a flurry of activities and programs that just keep people busy? Has she become involved in things to which God never called her? Has the message and mission of salvation of souls taken a back seat? Has her message in any way been compromised so as not to offend anyone at any time or in any way? Jesus certainly did not give in to that kind of thinking.

What if the parting words of Jesus, to go into all the world, preaching the good news, and making disciples of all men,[95] would be the litmus test for all the things we do? **What if** the Church would once again resurrect the purpose and instructions for her existence? **What if** we stormed Heaven day and night with prayers on behalf of souls? **What if** we would each focus on individuals that we know are lost and faithfully intercede for them with perseverance?

What if we would wake up each morning and say, "Lord, let at least one person who needs to hear Your good news cross my path today. Lord, give me the words to speak to them that will draw them to you. Let me love them with Your love." **What if** we approached each day with that as the cry of our heart? **What if** our eyes were opened and sensitive to the souls of men and women?

What if our hearts were so bonded with the heart of God that we cared more about the things He cares about than we did anything else?

God placed His own burden for Jerusalem upon Nehemiah. Had Nehemiah conceded to the lure of life in Persia, he may have easily dismissed the burden. Many of his fellow Jews had done so. The allure of a life of comfort erased memories of the homeland. The majority of exiles settled in to their new environment, severing connections of their past. Life in agricultural Persia was pleasant, safe, and enticing. Life in the palace where Nehemiah spent the majority of his time, had its own set of entrapments and temptations. Nehemiah was constantly surrounded by the beauty of the palace, the riches of palace life, and the entitlements that may have come from holding a respected position. It would have been easy to become accustomed to such a lifestyle. It would have been natural to settle for what was familiar. It would have been understandable if Nehemiah had chosen to live out his life surrounded by comfort and surrendering to the ordinary.

What if he had? **What if** his response to the report that Jerusalem was in disrepair and the people were living in disgrace was, "That's a shame, but what can I do about it?" **What if** he had valued his position above the needs of God's chosen city? **What if** he had given into the temptation to maintain and protect his comfort zone? **What if** he had been like many of his fellow Jews and regarded life in Persia as just too good to give up? **What if** he didn't want to give up the perks and comforts of palace employment? **What if** he had counted the cost of returning to Jerusalem as just too high to pay? **What if** the life he had grown accustomed to made him despise the thought of a long, hard, eight hundred mile journey? **What if** the thought of trading palace life for a life in a barren, dismal, and dismantled city made him say, "Forget it; not my problem?"

Then perhaps the walls of Jerusalem would not have been rebuilt. Or perhaps God would have raised up another to carry out the mission and Nehemiah would have never received God's blessing, and his name would not be remembered.

It appears none of those thoughts ever crossed Nehemiah's mind. It appears comfort and familiarity did not have a grip on him. It appears they were never on his radar screen. Thank God they were not.

Let's be honest here – ugly honest. We like our comforts in America. That is an undeniable and indisputable reality. One only need watch the commercials on television, see the ads in magazines, read the billboards on the highway, or stroll through a shopping mall to recognize that comfort is high on our priority list. We like temperatures to be pleasing; we like a food a certain way; we like to be served expediently; we like our computers to be lightning fast; we like our sheets to be at least six hundred thread count; we like our car seats either heated or cooled; we like our remote control at our fingertips; we like our lawns manicured; we like our homes well appointed; we want our pastors to give messages that make us feel good.

We are told "it is the good life," and that "we deserve it, we're worth it." But is it, and do we, and are we?

Comfort can be a wonderful thing; but it can also be a deception and a pitfall. It was for the Jewish exiles in Persia, and it can be for us today also. Comfort has the potential to lead us away from God. Comfort has the potential to make us complacent, lazy, falsely satisfied, self-righteous, and deceitfully contented.

When the Israelites first entered the Promised Land under the leadership of Joshua, God warned them through Moses about the danger of comfort.

Otherwise, when you eat and are satisfied, when you build fine homes and settle down, and when your herds and your flocks grow large and your silver and gold increase and all you have is multiplied, then your heart will become proud and you will forget the LORD your God, who brought you out of Egypt, out of the land of slavery. [96]

Jesus, as the risen and victorious King, speaks to the church of Laodicea,

You say, 'I am rich; I have acquired wealth and do not need a thing.' But you do not realize that you are wretched, pitiful, poor, blind, and naked. [97]

Of course comfort is not all bad, but **what if** we were to recognize the potential danger that sometimes accompanies it?

What if we would guard ourselves against its allure? **What if** we would refrain from being swayed by the commercials and advertisements that lie and tell us we need so much stuff? **What if** we realized comfort can lead us away from God? **What if** we realized it can cause our hearts to grow lukewarm in our relationship with Him? **What if** we realized comfort can cause us to worship ourselves, and not God? **What if** we could discern that comfort can become an idol to us? **What if** we comprehended that it is often the call of comfort that keeps us from doing what God wants us to do? **What if** we recognized that it is the appeal of comfort that keeps us from sacrificing for the sake of others and the sake of the Kingdom? **What if** we recognized that our drive for comfort is often fed by the god of self? **What if** we discerned the raging battle that exists between seeking comfort and dying to self? **What if** we understood that sometimes discomfort is really better for us than comfort? **What if** we understood that comfort can make us soft, vulnerable, and susceptible to compromise and sin? **What if** we understood that discomfort has the potential to make us grow, be appreciative, and become stronger within?

We would be free from a burden of unnecessary stuff, free from the bondage it puts us in, and free to willingly obey God. Maybe, as Nehemiah, we would more eagerly and readily pursue the plans and purposes God has for us.

Nehemiah obviously carried a burden for Jerusalem, but it was not until he actually heard the report that he knew how to pray. Sometimes God will just lay a person or a situation on our hearts; sometimes we need to inquire or obtain information in order to know what and how to pray. Once Nehemiah understood the condition, he immediately sought the Lord. He prayed earnestly day and night for God's intervention, forgiveness, wisdom, direction, and empowerment.

Nehemiah was what Mark Batterson would call a "circle maker." In his book, <u>Circle Maker,</u> Batterson tells the legend of a man named Honi who lived outside Jerusalem a century before the birth of Christ. The city was experiencing a drought that was resulting in famine in the land. People were sick and dying. One day, standing right outside the wall (the wall that Nehemiah had rebuilt two hundred years before!), Honi held a six-foot staff in his hand and began to turn like a math compass. He made a full circle. When he was finished, he dropped to his knees in the center of the circle, and with a voice of authority that was fortified by unwavering faith, Honi prayed:

"Lord of the universe, I swear before Your great name that I will not move from this circle until You have shown mercy upon Your children."[98]

Within moments, raindrops began to fall. The people rejoiced, but Honi continued to pray:

"Not for such rain have I prayed, but for rain that will fill cisterns, pits, and caverns."[99]

The people experienced a torrential downfall that day. The size of the raindrops, along with the volume and force of the rain, sent people running for cover from the flash floods. Again Honi prayed:

"Not for such rain have I prayed, but for rain of Your favor, blessing and graciousness."[100]

The rain changed from a torrent to a gentle, calm, peaceful yet steady downfall that soaked the ground. The people's hearts were also soaked and many who had lost their faith returned to the God of Israel.

How desperate we are today for people who will pray as Nehemiah and Honi did? **What if** we would pray as they did? **What if** we would intercede day and night? **What if** we would make circles around our concerns and lift them up before the Lord? **What if** we would persevere in our prayers until we received the answer? **What if** we would pray with unwavering faith, believing that He hears our prayers and believing He will answer them? **What if** we prayed standing upon His Word and His character? **What if** we prayed with boldness and authority? **What if** as we prayed, we also asked to be the vessel through which God might provide the answer? **What if** we were to pray BIG and believe BIG as both Nehemiah and Honi prayed?

Nehemiah did pray and believed BIG. Rebuilding the broken down wall of Jerusalem was no small undertaking. It was immense, monumental, mammoth, enormous, gigantic, and colossal. Although the first group that returned to Jerusalem in 538 BCE had started to rebuild the wall, they were unable to get very far in the task. Although the reconstruction of the temple had been completed and people had settled in, the walls of Jerusalem remained in shambles. The people faced defeat, discouragement and adversity at every attempt. Erecting any semblance of a wall to protect the city seemed hopeless. But Nehemiah was not deterred by any of that. He prayed big and he believed big because he served a God that was bigger than any of it. His faith was not in man, not in his own ability, but in His God. Within fifty-six days of his beginning the reconstruction, the wall was complete. Now that's BIG!

What if we prayed big? **What if** we believed big? **What if** we prayed and believed and acted as if our God was bigger than any of our problems? **What if** we believed that what is difficult for us is easy for Him? **What if** we were to lift before Him the broken things we try to carry but cannot fix: our broken marriages, our broken families, our broken government, our broken churches, our broken nation, and our broken world? **What if** we would stop wringing our hands in despair and lift them to Heaven in hope? **What if** we put all these things in the hands of the One who created the world? **What if** we stopped settling for the mediocre and believed for the extraordinary? **What if** we stopped settling for what is normal and contended for the supernatural? **What if** we were to throw off those things that weigh us down and raise our face to the God Who always does BIG things in a BIG way?

He's waiting for someone to believe Him for something BIG!

Father God, Maker of all creation, You Who are the Beginning and the End, You who holds all things in the palm of Your hands, You Who do all things well, God we cry out to You. Lord, there is brokenness all around us. And we confess that that brokenness is a result of our sin. Lord we again ask for Your forgiveness and mercy to be poured upon us. And we ask that You, Who are the healer of all things, would bring healing to the broken. We ask that You, Who are the repairer of the breach, would rebuild the walls of protection and blessing in our lives and the life of our nation. We ask that You, Who takes broken things and makes them whole, would bring health and wholeness again. We ask that You, Who alone brings dead things to life, would once again breathe Your life into our beings and our nation. Father, these are big things. No human is capable of doing any of them. Only You God can do the impossible. But we're asking big, and we're believing big, and we will continue until we receive Your answer. In Jesus' Name, Amen.

PERSONAL REFLECTION

1. Has God ever burdened your heart with a task for you to do? How did you respond? What happened?

2. What did the broken walls of Jerusalem really represent? What do you understand to be the correlation between "broken walls" and the brokenness in the lives of people? How is that applicable to our lives today?

3. What qualities of Nehemiah do you admire the most? How might his example affect you in your home or workplace?

4. Have you ever prayed and believed God for something BIG – something that could not possibly happen without His intervention? Would you select an area of our nation that desperately needs God's power released within it, and commit to pray for it?

5. What three **what ifs** spoke to you the most? Would you add any?

10
THE HIGH PRIESTLY PRAYER OF JESUS
John 17:1-26

As the pages of the Old Testament come to a close, the city of Jerusalem was once again inhabited, and its wall and temple were functional. None of them ever came close to the beauty and magnificence they had displayed before the Diaspora. The land no longer was a separate nation, but a territory that would be governed by outside forces for thousands of years. Those who left Persia returned to the land, but not necessarily to their God, at least not whole heartedly.

In most Christian Bibles the book of Nehemiah is located somewhere near the middle of the Old Testament. This can be slightly confusing. The confusion arises because the books are not arranged chronologically, but by category: the Pentateuch, historical books, writings, and prophets. Actually, the rebuilding of the wall under Nehemiah was the last significant event that occurred before the end of the Old Testament. Just a few years following the completion of the wall, the prophet Malachi spoke God's Word to His people.

Malachi's word was significant; it was direct, specific and strong. After all the people had been through, Malachi rebuked them for their continual waywardness and for their actions of contempt towards the Lord. But he ended God's final prophetic word with an encouragement that spoke of hope and promise.

"But for you who revere my name, the sun of righteousness will rise with healing in its wings. And you will go out and leap like calves released from the stall. Then you will trample down

the wicked; they will be ashes under the soles of your feet on the day when I do these things," says the Lord Almighty.[101]

"See, I will send you the prophet Elijah before the great and dreadful day of the LORD comes. He will turn the hearts of the fathers to their children, and the hearts of the children to their fathers; or else I will come and strike the land with a curse."[102]

A new day was coming.

Final word, and then God was silent.

Ponder that thought with me for a moment. It is profound. He, Who was The Word, spoke no word. He, Who spoke the world into being by His Word, was silent. He, Who had spoken for thousands of years to His people through the patriarchs, prophets, judges or kings, spoke no more. He, Who had revealed secrets through visions and dreams, gave no more visions or dreams. It was as if His holy mouth had been bolted shut.

Imagine what it must have been like for the people. Despite the fact that they rarely obeyed Him, they were still accustomed to the God of Israel directing them, disciplining them, stirring them with hope, and speaking words of correction, encouragement, or grace. For thousands of years He had spoken into their daily existence. They may not have realized it, but they were a people dependent on God's spoken Word to them.

Then nothing but silence from Heaven.

Initially they may have been delighted and relieved; much like a young person when they first get out from under the instruction and correction of their parents. But this silence lasted four hundred years. Four hundred long and barren years, when the Word of the Lord was absent from the land. Four hundred bleak years, when the people must have felt abandoned, desperate and lost.

These four hundred years are referred to as the Silent Years. Silent does not necessarily translate inactive. History records that much happened during this period. It was during this time that Alexander the Great ascended to power and the Grecian Empire came to the forefront. It was during this period that the Roman Empire achieved dominance over the region. The tiny piece of territory once known as Israel was greatly impacted by all these events. Yet during the upheavals, transference of power, and battles that went with them, God was silent.

The silence must have been deafening for those who longed for a Word.

Was God preparing the stage for The Word he was about to speak? Was He clearing the atmosphere to send forth the most dramatic and profound Word He had ever spoken? Was He causing hearts to be extraordinarily hungry for His Word? Was He intentionally causing spirits to thirst for a Word from Him? Was His silence intended to make This Word distinct from all the other words He had spoken? Was the silence to highlight the exceptional and extraordinary nature of The Word He had been preparing to send forth since before the foundation of the world?

After four hundred years, God once again spoke. We find the account in the first chapter of the book of Luke. Zechariah, a priest, drew his lot to appear before the Lord at the altar of incense in the temple. While he was there, an angel named Gabriel appeared to him and broke the silence. Scripture says Zechariah was "startled and gripped with fear."[103] I imagine so; you would have been too, and so would I.

Gabriel spoke to Zechariah and told him that he and his wife, Elizabeth, were going to have a child. This news was about as unbelievable to Zechariah as the same sort of message had been to Abraham and Sarah. Both couples were elderly and well beyond child bearing years.

Try to imagine what this encounter must have been like for Zechariah. First, angelic appearances were neither normal nor conventional. Second, ageing couples did not ordinarily conceive and give birth. Third, and perhaps most astounding, God had not uttered a word in four hundred years. No word. Nothing. Not a whisper is recorded.

Yet Gabriel, angel of the Most High, was speaking to Zechariah as if it were an everyday occurrence. No wonder Zechariah lost his ability to speak. There is a profound lesson in this interaction. When God speaks, what does man have to say? When God speaks, what can man say? When God speaks, man should be quiet, listen, ponder, and obey.

Gabriel's message to Zechariah picked up right where Malachi had left off four hundred years before. The Old Testament prophet's final words were that God would send someone like the prophet Elijah to prepare the way of the Lord's coming. God broke the silence of four hundred years with a message to Zechariah concerning the birth of this forerunner. To God it was as if no time had elapsed! God is eternal and timeless.

Can you imagine being the first person to whom God spoke after four hundred years? What kind of thoughts must have run through his mind? "Does God still speak? Am I hallucinating? Is someone playing some kind of trick? Who am I that an angel would speak to me? Why me? Will anyone believe this?" What kind of emotions must have gripped his heart? Can you imagine the awe, confusion, fear, surprise, delight, wonder, and excitement that came with the realization that God was once again speaking – and he was speaking to YOU? Can you imagine what anticipation must have spread among the people?

God was preparing the stage for The Word He was about to send forth.

Once the silence was broken, God continued to speak. Again He dispatched Gabriel - this time to a town in Nazareth, to a young woman, named Mary, who was betrothed to a man named Joseph. The message was similar to the one delivered to Zechariah in that it concerned the conception and birth of a Child. But, at the same time, it was drastically different.

The manner in which this Child would be conceived was incomprehensible to human thinking. If an elderly couple giving birth to a child was improbable, then the method of conception for Mary's child was implausible. This Child would be conceived within its mother's womb in a manner no other child before or since was conceived. From beginning to end, this would be no ordinary or typical pregnancy. This Baby would be formed in Mary's virgin womb as the Holy Spirit of God overshadowed Mary. This One would be Immanuel, God with us, the very Son of God Himself.

This message not only broke the silence, it shook the foundations of hell; it declared war on the domain of darkness, and it shattered the strongholds that had held mankind in bondage for generations.

If Zechariah was astounded by the message given him by Gabriel, imagine what Mary must have experienced! Can we possibly identify with the explosion of wonder, apprehension, joy, and exhilaration within her young heart and spirit?

With the silence broken, so much began to happen! God was setting the stage, preparing the way, laying the foundation for the greatest expression of His Word to be revealed.

Zechariah and Elizabeth did conceive, just as Gabriel had said. Their baby, John, grew into the one whose message was, "Prepare the way of the Lord."

Mary did conceive, just as Gabriel had said. Her child, Jesus, was The Living Word. He was, and is, and always will be, the utmost articulation of God to man.

In the beginning was the Word and the Word was with God, and the Word was God. He was with God in the beginning. Through him all things were made; without him nothing was made that has been made. In him was life, and that life was the light of men. The light shines in the darkness, but the darkness has not understood it.[104]

The Word became flesh and made his dwelling among us.[105]

All the patriarchs, prophets, priests, and kings who had gone before pointed to this Promised One. Their lives foreshadowed his ministry and mission. Their messages prophesized His coming. For He, Jesus the Christ, Immanuel, God with us, was the ultimate and eternal Patriarch, Priest, Prophet and King.

Jesus walked on planet Earth in His flesh tent for thirty-some years. In comparison to average life spans, that is a relatively short time, even in biblical history. For the majority of those years he must have lived a rather quiet, uneventful, and ordinary life, for very little is recorded. But in three years – three very brief years – he turned the world and all of history upside down.

He burst upon a humanity that had been starving for the voice of God for hundreds of years. When He spoke His teachings pierced the hearts of men and women with truth. His prayers released power from on high. His miracles were undeniable. His integrity was beyond reproach. His confidence was unshakeable. His authority was commanding. His touch brought healing to the blind, the lame, the crippled, and the leper. A simple word from His lips sent demons running and those in bondage free. He accomplished more in three brief years than any other person who has ever lived has accomplished in a lifetime.

He was born in an obscure village, the child of a peasant woman. He grew up in another obscure village where he worked in a carpenter shop until he was thirty when public opinion turned against him.

He never wrote a book. He never held an office. He never went to college. He never visited a big city. He never traveled more than two hundred miles from the place where he was born. He did none of these things usually associated with greatness. He had no credentials but himself.

He was only thirty three. His friends ran away. One of them denied him. He was turned over to his enemies and went through the mockery of a trial. He was nailed to a cross between two thieves. While dying, his executioners gambled for his clothing the only property he had on earth.

When he was dead He was laid in a borrowed grave through the pity of a friend.

Nineteen centuries have come and gone and today Jesus is the central figure of the human race and the leader of mankind's progress. All the armies that have ever marched, all the navies that have ever sailed, all the parliaments that have ever sat, all the kings that have ever reigned put together have not affected the life of mankind on Earth as powerfully as that one solitary life.[106]

However, all that He did, all that He accomplished in those three brief years, does not compare to His one act of sacrifice upon the cross. It was for the cross that He left His throne in Heaven to be wrapped in swaddling clothes and laid in a manger on Earth. Without the cross, He would be remembered as a great teacher, a kind and compassionate man, and a worker of miracles.

But the cross made Him Savior, as He took ALL of the punishment that was rightfully ours upon Himself. The cross made Him Lord, as He rose from the death that the cross had inflicted. The cross made Him Victor, as He battled the enemy who brings death, and won. The cross made Him King, as he reclaimed the rights of mankind that Satan had usurped from Adam and Eve in the Garden.

Mankind looked upon the cross as a symbol of disgrace, disdain, shame, torture, and death. Jesus looked upon it as a vehicle to his destination of victory!

Jesus spent the night before His death with His disciples. From beginning to end, this was no ordinary night. Jesus began the evening by washing the disciples' feet. They were bewildered that their Master would assume the position of a servant.

Then he began the traditional Jewish Passover meal with them. The meal was celebrated once a year, and was a remembrance of God's deliverance of the Jewish people from the bondage of slavery in Egypt thousands of years before.

The disciples were all good Jews. Their ancestors had celebrated the Passover meal for generations. As young boys they had probably attended rabbinic training where they learned the proper wording and procedure for the Passover meal. They had probably celebrated the meal every year of their lives. They had probably celebrated at least two Passover meals with Jesus. They could probably recite the Passover program word for word, line by line. The format was set in stone – or so they thought. Imagine their confusion when He Who was The Word altered the traditional wording.

Imagine their astonishment when he held up the bread and said, "This is My body given for you." If they had not been paying attention before, they were then. Imagine their shock, as He held up the third cup of wine, known as the Cup of Redemption, and said, "This is My blood shed for you." Can you picture their perplexed and quizzical expressions as they looked at Him and one another, wondering what was He doing, and what in the world was He was talking about? The atmosphere must have been charged with the sense that everything was about to change. This was an intense moment. This was an important moment. This was a serious moment.

Jesus continued His discourse with them as they finished the meal and proceeded across the Kidron Valley to the Garden of Gethsemane. His demeanor must have been solemn; his words were contemplative. He realized He only had a short time remaining to share the matters most important to Him. His heart was burdened, not so much for what He knew He was facing, but for what He knew His friends were facing. They were unaware, and unprepared. He spent those final moments equipping them for what lay ahead.

He spoke of His impending death, eternal life, and the ministry of the coming Holy Spirit. He plainly explained that He and the Father were One, and the need for them to abide in Him. He spoke words of comfort, assurance, and truth into and over the disciples. (Judas, the betrayer, was not privy to these words; he had already departed to hand over the One who had loved him so much.)

And then he prayed. No other prayer is as powerful as this prayer of Jesus; not the prayer of Abraham, or Moses, or David, or Solomon, or Hezekiah, or Daniel, or Nehemiah, or any other prayer in Scripture. This was the high priestly prayer of the eternal High Priest Himself. This was the prayer which the One Who sits at the right hand of the Father prayed before He left Earth.

"Father, the time has come. Glorify your Son, that your Son may glorify you. For you granted him authority over all people that he might give eternal life to all those you have given him. Now this is eternal life: that they may know you, the only true God, and Jesus Christ, whom you have sent. I have brought you glory on earth by completing the work you gave me to do. And now, Father, glorify me in your presence with the glory I had with you before the world began.

"I have revealed you to those whom you gave me out of the world. They were yours; you gave them to me and they have obeyed your word. Now they know that everything you have given me comes from you. For I gave them the words you gave me and they accepted them. They knew with certainty that I came from you, and they believed that you sent me. I pray for them. I am not praying for the world, but for those you have given me, for they are yours. All I have is yours, and all you have is mine. And glory has come to me through them. I will remain in the world no longer, but they are still in the world, and I am coming to you. Holy Father, protect them by the power of your name – the name you gave me – so that they may be one as we are one. While I was with them, I protected them and kept them safe by that name you gave me. None has been lost except the one doomed to destruction so that Scripture would be fulfilled.

"I am coming to you now, but I say these things while I am still in the world, so that they may have the full measure of my joy within them. I have given them your word and the world has hated them, for they are not of the world any more than I am of the world. My prayer is not that you take them out of the world but that you protect them from the evil one. They are not

of the world, even as I am not of it. Sanctify them by the truth; your word is truth. As you sent me into the world, I have sent them into the world. For them I sanctify myself, that they too may be truly sanctified.

"My prayer is not for them alone. I pray also for those who will believe in me through their message, that all of them may be one, Father, just as you are in me and I am in you. May they also be in us so that the world may believe that you have sent me. I have given them the glory that you gave me, that they may be one as we are one. I in them and you in me. May they be brought to complete unity to let the world know that you sent me and have loved them even as you have loved me.

"Father, I want those you have given me to be with me where I am, and to see my glory, the glory you have given me because you loved me before the creation of the world.

"Righteous Father, though the world does not know you, I know you, and they know that you have sent me. I have made you known to them, and will continue to make you known in order that the love you have for me may be in them and that I myself may be in them."[107]

It is with fear and trepidation that I approach this prayer. How does one critique such a prayer? How does one analyze a prayer of Jesus? We don't; we can't – at least not with any measure of adequacy. Should not our response simply be to lift our hands and worship? Should not our reaction be one of sincere gratefulness?

Yet there are things woven into this prayer that we must comprehend. It is imperative if we are to live the life Jesus prayed for us to live. Every word was of grave importance to Him, and so it must be to us. This prayer was basically the last words Jesus spoke to his disciples.

If you have ever spent time with someone who is facing death, you know that they do not waste their time or breath on insignificant chatter. You know the words they choose are calculated and of substance to them. You know that what they say is meant to make an impression on those who hear. They use the time they have to pass on the essence of who they are and what is most important to them; they express their hopes and intentions for those left behind.

Jesus' high priestly prayer encompasses all of that.

As Jesus began to pray, He asked the Father to glorify Him. This request was totally devoid of selfish intent. The request was completely motivated by Jesus' desire to glorify the Father. He viewed His life as being so intricately entwined with the Father that everything He was and did pointed back to God. This is the way He conducted His life on Earth. Every word He spoke, every movement He made, every miracle He performed, every story or parable He told, and every life He touched was to glorify the Father. Even facing His excruciating crucifixion, His desire was to glorify God.

What if we desired to glorify the Father as Jesus did? **What if** bringing him glory was the underlying motive of everything we did? **What if** we evaluated everything we did or said on the basis of whether it brought God glory? **What if** we were less concerned about the attention and approval we receive? **What if** we were more concerned about how our actions reflect upon Him? **What if** we were more concerned with His reputation among men than our own? **What if** asking God to bless something was not because deep down we wanted to look good? **What if** our seeking His favor upon a ministry in which we were involved had nothing to do with us, but was completely about His glory? **What if** we were not so concerned with the accolades we might accumulate? **What if** we didn't measure the success of something by how much it might improve our lives? **What if** we were willing to "look bad" if it meant God received the glory? **What if** we were willing not to get the credit for something we may have done, and let God get the glory? **What if** we were willing to be misunderstood, ridiculed, and rejected if it meant God was glorified? Jesus certainly was. **What if** we were willing to suffer hardship, persecution, and possibly death if God ended up being glorified through our sacrifice? Jesus and the martyrs throughout the ages did just that.

A large portion of Jesus' glorifying the Father was demonstrated through his battle with Satan. I John 3:8 says, *"The reason the Son of God appeared was to destroy the devil's work."* Throughout His days on earth, everything Jesus did was to defeat the work of the enemy. Whether it was exposing the enemy's lies by teaching truth, setting captives free through deliverance, or casting out the spirit of infirmity, Jesus' very presence on Earth was a declaration of war against the domain of Satan. Jesus was fully cognizant of the war in the spiritual world between Good and evil, Light and dark, Holiness and sin. He was also painfully aware that before the next sunset He would be engaged in the war of all wars in the spiritual realm.

His high priestly prayer reflected that ongoing warfare. Jesus asked the Father to protect the disciples, and us, from the ensnarement of the enemy. Recognizing that He would no longer be physically present with them to protect them from the deceiver, He implored God to keep them with His sustaining power. Knowing that they would shortly be sent out into the world, He asked the Father to keep them separated from the lure of worldly seductions. In essence, He was asking His Father to put an invisible impenetrable wall around those who belonged to Him, to shield them from Satan's insidious tactics.

Knowing that Jesus' prayer was not just for the disciples at that time, but for all who bear His Name, prompts a sigh of relief from deep within me. It is indeed reassuring and comforting to claim His prayer as a covering in every believer's life. But we cannot simply rest in that prayer and be complacent to the war around us. It is a warfare that we may not be able to see with our physical eyes, but it is a war that is very much present. Its obscurity to our physical senses makes it even more dangerous, for we are often oblivious to it. We often go about our daily lives unaware of the enemy's lurking; we are often ignorant of his tactics; we are often blindsided by his plans and agendas against us. We are often lulled to sleep, unsuspecting that Satan is a roaring lion seeking whom he might devour.[108]

How many lives have been destroyed because their guard was down? Or worse yet, how many have been left defenseless because they have questioned the reality of the warfare? How many how been deceived into believing that Satan is not real, or at best is merely a cartoon figure with a pitchfork?

Jesus understood the reality of the warfare. He spoke about it, prayed about it, fought against it, and died to be victorious over it. He minced no words when he said the enemy has come to steal, kill and destroy.[109]

What if we were to grasp the reality of this war in the spiritual realm? **What if** we were to ask God to give us the spirit of discernment that we might see it more clearly? **What if** we were to take it more seriously than we do? **What if** we were to recognize the tactics the enemy uses? **What if** we were to become more proficient in defeating him? **What if** we were to identify the strongholds of the enemy and learn to use the weapons we have been given to demolish them?[110] **What if** we were to consciously and deliberately put on the armor of God[111] that we have been given? **What if** we were more skilled in our use of the Word of God as our weapon against the enemy? **What if** we more fully understood the authority we have to defeat him? **What if** we understood the principles of binding and loosening in the spiritual realm?[112] **What if** we followed the example of Jesus to speak to the demonic with authority and conviction? **What if** we embraced the gift and power of prayer to overcome the enemy? **What if** we lived our lives as Jesus did – to defeat the works of the evil one?

What if we prayed protection over those in our lives as Jesus did, and does, for us? **What if** every day we covered our spouses, our children, our neighbors, our co-workers, our friends, our fellow church members, our community leaders, our government leaders, and anyone else God brings to mind with prayer? **What if** we asked God to keep them with His sustaining power and protect them from the destructive plans of Satan? **What if** we asked Him to put an invisible impenetrable wall around them that no harm could come to them? **What if** we interceded on their behalf that they would be strong in the face of worldly temptation? **What if** we specifically declared war on the onslaught of drugs, alcohol, pornography, and all sorts of addictions that enslave so many in our generation?

The principle of unity is essential if we are to be effective in this warfare. Jesus understood that. In His prayer He referred to the unity that exists between the Father, the Son, and the Holy Spirit. The Three-In-One move in total and perfect unity. Each is individual in Their identity and purpose, but They are also woven together in flawless harmony. There is no dissension, no disequilibrium, and no division between them. There is no competition, no jealousy, and no undermining of one another. There is only uninterrupted oneness that translates into love, unity, peace and power. That is the example Jesus holds before us to emulate.

Yet His prayer goes even beyond our following this example. His prayer invites us to enter into the very oneness of the Father, Son, and Holy Spirit. He summons us to become one with Them so that we may extend that oneness to one another. As we experience that oneness with one another we bring glory to the Father. It is an ongoing circle of unity that flows from the Triune God to us and back to Him.

Jesus never asked for uniformity; He prayed for unity. The two are distinctly different. Uniformity negates the beauty of individuality. That was never what God intended. He created each one of us unique. He specializes in uniqueness. We are to celebrate our individuality and uniqueness, while also striving to exhibit unity despite our differences.

What if we purposed to understand that unity? **What if** we responded to the glorious invitation to join in the oneness the Father, Son and Holy Spirit share? **What if** we "made every effort to keep the unity of the Spirit through the bond of peace"?[113] **What if** we endeavored to make this prayer of Jesus a reality in our everyday living? **What if** we developed the skill of maintaining and celebrating our individual uniqueness, while contending for unity amidst our differences?

Jesus knew the blessings that flow from unity. He also knew the destructiveness of division. He witnessed Satan deceive a third of the angels of Heaven so that they were cast out. He watched as Satan stole the blissful harmony of Adam and Eve. He saw hatred enter the heart of Cain so that he killed his own brother Abel. He watched as generation after generation of mankind succumbed to the spirit of division and disunity. The fruit was always destruction and Satan was always at the helm.

As we look around our world today, there is ample evidence that the spirit of division is running rampant, and the fruit it produces is never good. Fifty percent of covenant marriages end in divorce. Parents and children are at odds with one another. Church splits seem to be the norm. Violence runs rampant in cities. Government elections are bitter and hateful. Demonstrations have become increasingly fierce and aggressive. Online comments are often vicious. Threats between nations have become progressively more hostile and concerning. There is not a day when rebellion, dissension, and divisiveness do not enter our homes through the news on our televisions. The intensity and speed of all of these matters are rapidly accelerating. They make our world unsafe, unstable, and insecure.

This is not going to end well.

Jesus said, *"Every kingdom divided against itself will be ruined, and every city or household divided against itself will not stand."*[114] The fruit of division is not good. There is no question that division is a demonic force that will destroy everything in its path. It is toxic; it is deadly; and it is oh so present in our world today.

Our nation cannot continue down the path paved with division. If she does, America will not survive. She will destroy herself from within.

What if we would just realize that any time we see division it is an indication that Satan is at work? **What if** we would purpose in our hearts to not participate in any divisive behavior? **What if** we would be more proactive in promoting unity? **What if** we would be ministers of reconciliation in situations where oneness was threatened? **What if** we would avail ourselves to be peace makers in these situations? **What if** we would guard our mouths from speaking any words that might breed discord or division?

What if we would diligently safeguard our marriages? **What if** we would peacefully work through issues in our personal relationships? **What if** we contend for authentic unity within churches and the Church as a whole? **What if** we would be fierce in protecting the unity of the Spirit?

What if we would pray that our government officials could work together in unity despite their differences? **What if** they committed to working for the good of our country, and not their own agendas? **What if** we focused more on the things that bind us together rather than the things that divide? **What if** we ceased seeing others as our enemy, but rather as fellow brothers and sisters in God?

What if instead of holding up protest signs, we would hold up the Word of God? **What if** instead of holding our fists up in resistance, we would fold them in prayer? **What if** instead of shouting at one another, we listened for a change? **What if** instead of trying to prove our point, we treated the opinions of others with respect? **What if** we realized that none of us has all the answers, but we all have a piece, and when we allow the pieces to come together we get a fuller picture?

What if instead of turning our backs on one another we would turn our faces in unity toward God?

Jesus prayed this prayer over two thousand years ago on the night He was arrested and betrayed. Unity was dear to His heart. It is a sad commentary that it is the only prayer of Jesus that is yet to be fulfilled. In two thousand years, mankind has not figured out how to surrender so this prayer might come to fruition. Perhaps it will not come to pass until Heaven comes to

Earth at the end of time. But Jesus prayed it that fateful night for the "then." He prayed it also for the "now."

What if we would join Jesus and make it the prayer of our hearts in our time?

Lord, let it be so.

Heavenly Father, Precious Jesus, and Blessed Holy Spirit, thank You for this prayer of our High Priest. Thank You that He covered us with this prayer and blessing. Lord, forgive us that we have not been obedient nor walked in the ways of His prayer. Forgive us that we so often take the glory that belongs to You for ourselves. Forgive us that we have not recognized the warfare in the spiritual realm, and we have not taken up our weapons to defeat the enemy of our souls. Forgive us that we have not understood the imperativeness of contending for unity. Forgive us when we have spoken or done things that have fostered division. Father, we so desperately need your intervention in our world today. We need Your peace and unity to invade our marriages, our families, our churches, our schools, our governments, our nations. Raise us up as vessels through which You can bring unity to situations of discord. Your Word says, "Blessed are the peacemakers." Lord, may we bring peace where there is chaos. May we bring oneness where there is division. May we bring the sweet fragrance of Jesus to those around us. May we allow His high priestly prayer to be fulfilled in our lives. In His precious Name, Amen.

PERSONAL REFLECTION

1. Have you ever experienced a time when you felt God was silent? What was it like?

2. In your heart of hearts, are there ways or times you care more about the accolades or approval you may receive than the glory your life brings to God?

3. How have you safeguarded the people in your life from the enemy's agenda against them?

4. Are you a person who brings discord or unity to your home, community, and/or church? Are there ways you can be a peacemaker, or bring unity where you see division?

4. What is your understanding of the difference between unity and uniformity?

5. What are your thoughts that Jesus' prayer for unity is the only prayer He prayed that is yet to be fulfilled?

6. Which three **what ifs** spoke to you the most? Would you add any?

11
OUR WATCH

Jesus' high priestly prayer had been for the benefit of His disciples. When He finished, He sought a quiet and solitary place to be alone with His Father. He knew His strength came from His communion with God. It was not the company of man He sought at this moment, but utter and absolute union with His Father. He was well aware that no one could go with Him on the journey He was about to take. This final assignment of His life on Earth was His and His alone. His mother would watch from afar; His disciples would watch from hiding; even His Heavenly Father would abandon Him for a span of time.

The depth of anguish and despair He experienced was truly beyond comprehension. Even before His arrest, He agonized over what was to come. Luke, the only Gentile author in the Bible, records that while in the Garden Jesus sweat drops of blood.[115] The Gospel of Luke is the only gospel to record this fact. Perhaps that is because Luke was a physician and was observant of such physical details.

Sweating drops of blood is a highly unusual condition, but a medically verifiable and explainable disorder. It is called hematohidrosis. Under extreme mental, emotional, or physical pressure, the blood vessels surrounding one's sweat glands will constrict. Then, when the anxiety passes, the blood vessels dilate and rupture. The blood enters the sweat glands, and as the person begins to sweat, the blood is pushed out through the pores. This is a rare condition and only occurs in times of dire stress.[116]

This was merely the beginning of Jesus' ordeal. Within hours of sharing the Passover meal with His disciples, He was arrested. Less than twenty-four hours after His high priestly prayer, He stood unjustly accused before the religious and political leaders of the day. He endured the mockery of an illegal trial. He was scourged and beaten. His flesh was torn beyond recognition. He was sentenced to the death of a criminal. He was nailed to a wooden cross. He died from asphyxiation[117] and a broken heart. His ravaged, disfigured, and bloodless body was laid in a tomb.

Despite knowing ahead of time that all of this would happen, Jesus' agony in the Garden was offset by an even greater peace and joy. Hebrews 12:2 says, *"For the joy set before Him, He endured the cross..."*

What was that joy set before Him? Knowing that He was about to strike a fatal blow to the Enemy; knowing that He would be victorious over sin, Hell, and the grave; knowing that He would be trading His earthly body for a heavenly body; knowing that He would be reunited with His Father as He was raised to sit at His right hand; ... **and...... us.**

We were the joy set before Him. Knowing that His victory would overflow onto us gave Him the strength, conviction, motive and power to endure the cross. Knowing that His victory would mean forgiveness, freedom, healing, restoration, and victory for us filled Him with purpose and determination. Knowing that we would be released from Satan's grip stirred anticipation within Him. Knowing that the relationship between God and man, which had been shattered in the Garden of Eden, would be reestablished flooded His spirit with joy.

Can you imagine His face when He burst forth from the tomb that first resurrection morning? Can you picture the look of triumph? Can you visualize the smile of sweet victory? Can you hear the deep belly laughter of delight? Can you imagine the unabashed pleasure in knowing the purpose for His coming to Earth was complete? Can you envision the glorious light of Heaven emanating from Him?

Mission accomplished!

Can you conceive of the longing within Him to reveal Himself to the disciples? Can you imagine His pleasure, and maybe even a tad of gleeful amusement, as He contemplated their responses?

He appeared to them many times over the next forty days.[118] He walked with them and continued to teach and prepare them. Then, He left them again, as He rose to take His rightful and victorious place at the right hand of His Father in Heaven.

I am always amazed at how Scripture can sometimes be devoid of details. For me, this is one of those times. Can you imagine the disciples' complete amazement as they watched His feet leave the earth and His body ascend in the clouds? After all the miracles they had witnessed, this still had to be astonishing, astounding, and staggering!

As He made this dramatic exit of all exits, He left His disciples with the mission to carry on His work, to pick up where He had left off, and to spread the message to all mankind through all the ages. He did not leave them orphaned to accomplish the work on their own. He sent the Holy Spirit to indwell them, direct them, and empower them.

That was their mission. That was their time. That was their watch.

Now it's our mission. Now it's our time. Now it's our watch.

Acts 17:26 says, *"From one man he made every nation of men, that they should inhabit the whole earth; and he determined the times set for them and the exact places where they should live. God did this so that men would seek him and perhaps reach out for him and find him."*

If you are reading this book, I am going to assume that you are alive. According to this Scripture, God has determined this time in history for you, for me, and for us. It is not happenstance that you were born in this period of history. Not only that, but Ephesians 2:10 says, *"For we are God's workmanship created in Christ Jesus to do good works, which God prepared in advance for us to do."* If we put these two scriptures together we can conclude that God has placed each one of us in the location where we live, and in the time in which we live, so that He may do the good works through us that He has destined us to accomplish.

Each and every life has a purpose. Each and every life has abundant potential. Each and every life is filled with boundless promise. Each and every life has a God-ordained destiny.

What if each one of us believed God created us teeming with purpose, potential, and promise? **What if** each one of us believed God has good works that are specific to us? **What if** we endeavored to discover what they are? **What if** we purposed in our hearts to accomplish them? **What if** we discarded the numerous distractions in our lives and focused on God's purposes? **What if** we availed ourselves to God that He might achieve His purposes through us? **What if** we set our course so that God's goals were our goals?

Isn't that what Abraham, Moses, David, Solomon, Hezekiah, Daniel, and Jesus did? Isn't that what other patriarchs, kings, and prophets did? Did not each one of them step into a God appointment that was assigned to them?

In the time that was assigned to them, they were history makers and history changers. They brought the situations of their day and age to their God in prayer, inviting His will and power to intersect their lives, and trusting Him to intervene. In each instance they recognized the dire condition man had created by his own sin. In each instance they relied upon the promises and covenants of God. In each instance they called upon His awesome, gracious, and merciful character to prevail over the consequences of their own doing.

In each instance it was *one* person praying. In each instance it was *one* person of faith who stood upon the promises of God. In each instance it was *one* person who trusted in the character of God. In each instance it was *one* person who dared to humbly yet boldly lay his request before God. In each instance it was *one* person who interceded on the behalf of others. In each instance it was *one* person who knew that God was their one and only hope. In each instance it was *one* person – *just one*

In each instance God was faithful. In each instance He heard and received their prayer. In each instance He answered.

He always does. He always will. That is Who He Is.

Jeremiah 5:1 says, *"Roam the streets of Jerusalem, look around and consider, search through her squares! If you can find a person, if there is one who does justice, who seeks truth, then I will pardon the city."*

Is it possible that God is looking for those "one persons" today? Is it possible that the eyes of the Lord still go throughout the earth looking for those whose hearts are right toward Him?[119] Is it possible He is still looking for those who will stand in the gap?[120] Is it possible He still desires those who will garb themselves in the armor of God and declare warfare in the spiritual realm?[121]

The answer is YES! - Undeniably, irrefutably, and resoundingly YES! We need the intervention of God as much as– probably more so – as any other time in history. There is not one facet of life that is exempt from needing God's Presence and power.

As a result of our sin, America is taking a parallel path to the one Israel took in the times of the patriarchs, kings, and prophets. America is on a downward spiral which is accelerating with increasing speed. She has allowed injustices to prevail, sin to be legalized, morals to be corrupted, perversions to be accepted, and spiritual lukewarmness to become the norm.

Deuteronomy 8:8-9 reads as if it is a description of America.

For the LORD is bringing you into a good land – a land of streams and pools of water, with springs flowing in the valley and hills; a land with wheat and barley, vines and fig trees, pomegranates, olive oil and honey; a land where bread will not be scarce and you will lack nothing; a land where the rocks are iron and you can dig copper out of the hills.

This is a description of a rich land, a lavish and fruitful land, a beautiful and abundant land. But it is not a description of America; it is the description of Israel. It is the description of Israel before years of sin, disobedience, and waywardness ravaged the land. It is a description of a land that was lavishly blessed before plagues, disease, droughts, invasions, and war raped it of its beauty and fruitfulness.

In 1867, the author Mark Twain visited the region that was once known as the nation of Israel. This was his assessment of the land:

...a desolate country whose soil is rich enough, but is given over wholly to weeds – a silent mournful expanse...A desolation is here that not even imagination can grace with the

pomp of life and action...We never saw a human being on the whole route...There was hardly a tree or shrub anywhere. Even the olive and the cactus, those friends of worthless soil, had almost deserted the country.[122]

The consequences of sin are far reaching and devastating. As we look across this great nation of ours, we are astounded by its beauty, its abundance, and its natural wonders. America has indeed been blessed by the Creator. But she is not immune to God's discipline, and she is not excused from the effects of sin and disobedience. If God would allow His beloved Israel to be vanquished because of her continual unrepentant sin, let us not think that America will escape His discipline. It is hard to imagine Mark Twain's description of Israel being applicable to America, but God's character does not change. He is longsuffering, but He will not tolerate blatant continual sin forever.

Not that long ago, President Ronald Reagan called for America to be a kinder, gentler nation. In recent years she has unfortunately become quite the opposite. President Reagan challenged America to be a city on a hill whose light burned brightly. That light is rapidly growing dimmer. Without the intervention of God, America's destination will be the same as Israel's and Judah's of the Old Testament. It did not end well for them.

But the prayers we have examined tell us it doesn't have to end that way. The prayers we have examined prove that prayer does make a difference. The prayers we have examined show that our God answers prayers. He delights in answering them. The prayers we have examined are evidence that prayers can change the path of a person, a nation, and a world. Prayers founded in faith release miracles and hope.

This is our watch. What will we do with it?

What if we would earnestly contend for souls we do not know, whose faces we have never seen, who are on a path of destruction? That's what Abraham did. **What if** we would faithfully intercede for those we do know, but are choosing a life of sin over a life of obedience and righteousness? That's what Moses did. **What if** our leaders desired the Presence of the Lord, and His guidance over our nation, as David did? **What if** our leaders would pray for our nation and her people, as Solomon did? **What if** our leaders would fast, pray, and turn their heads to God in times of crisis and warfare? **What if** they were to rely on the power of God more than they did man's ability and efforts for our protection? That's what Hezekiah did. **What if** all of us would purpose in our hearts not to defile ourselves by the worldliness around us? **What if** we lived our lives with such purity and resolve that God would reveal His plans and secrets to us? That's the life that Daniel lived. **What if** we would allow our hearts to be broken with what breaks the heart of God? **What if** we would mourn for the brokenness around us and be vessels through which God can bring wholeness? That's what Nehemiah did. **What if** we would yearn for the power of the Holy Spirit to be released in our lives and across this nation? **What if** we were to cease participating in divisive measures and contend for unity in every aspect of our lives? That was Jesus' prayer. **What if** His prayer for unity came to pass under our watch?

In Jeremiah 29:7, the prophet admonishes the people to pray for the peace and prosperity of the city in which they lived. **What if** throughout every city in America, believers were faithful in praying for its peace and prosperity? **What if** in your city, you would faithfully pray for peace and prosperity?

I Timothy 2:1-4 says, *I urge, first of all, that requests, prayers, intercession and thanksgiving be made for everyone –*

for kings and all those in authority, that we may live peaceful and quiet lives in all godliness and holiness. This is good, and pleases God our savior, who wants all men to be saved and to come to a knowledge of the truth.

Notice that Timothy is not suggesting; he is urging. The word conveys weightiness and emphasis to what is being said. Notice that the call for prayer is the first thing he says, again implying importance. Notice that he includes all in authority, not just some. At the time of Timothy's writing, the governing authorities were not very favorable to Christians. Timothy is saying that we need to pray not just for those with whom we agree, but for all in positions of authority. Notice that the result of such prayer is peace, godliness, and holiness. Notice that such prayer is pleasing to God, and will draw men to a saving knowledge of Jesus Christ.

Free speech is a beautiful right we have as citizens of a great nation. But it is not just a right and privilege; it also carries with it a responsibility. As I write this closing chapter, hate, rebellion, and borderline anarchy are sweeping across our nation. Instead of heeding the instruction in the Word of God to pray for our officials, there is a movement to undermine, harass, criticize, and discredit. The end result will be chaos and destruction. We cannot disobey God's Word and expect to have a happy ending.

What if we would take God at His Word and lift those in authority over us in prayer? This does not mean we need to cease sharing our concerns with them, but it does mean we need to couple that sharing with prayer.

If it only takes *one* praying in faith, power, and authority to move the heart and hand of God, think of what a multitude of prayers before His heavenly throne would do! I believe the Spirit of God is calling for an army of spiritual warriors to rise up and take their positions. The Spirit bids us to cast off the comforts and excuses that hinder us from being effective soldiers in the spiritual war that is all around us. We are to garb ourselves with the full armor of truth, faith, righteousness, peace, and salvation. We are to be armed with the Word of God and empowered by the indwelling Presence of the Holy Spirit.

The Spirit cries, "Rise up, army of the Living God!" Now is the time. Now is our watch. Now is the time to enter a new level of war in the spiritual realm. Now is the time to be serious, committed, and steadfast in prayer. Now is the time to throw off all constraints.

The forces of hell are advancing as never before. They have been unleashed in fierceness and magnitude. This is our watch against them. There are those who must take their stand as watchmen against the coming onslaught. There are those who must know how to wield the sword of the Spirit. We must leave no post unmanned, no wall unprotected.

In the midst of the darkness, God has not left us without light. In the midst of confusion, God has not left us without a strategy. In the midst of despair, He has not left us without hope. And in the midst of disappointment, He has not left us without promise.

The Spirit is sending forth a battle cry. Who will answer the call? Who will rise up in courage and faith? Who will give no place to discouragement?

The battle is raging in the spiritual realm as never before. Heaven is waiting for a battle cry to ascend from earth in response to the battle cry from the Spirit. Who will lift up the cry? The angelic armies of Heaven are waiting for the army on Earth to lift up the battle cry in prayer. Who will take their position on their knees to entreat Heaven for victory?

This is the time into which we were born. This is our watch. **What if** each one of us would hear the cry of God's Spirit to rise up as a mighty army against the forces of darkness? **What if** we would understand that repentance of our sin is an essential part of warfare? **What if** we lifted our voices in worship before God as a part of our warfare? **What if** we were to walk in the power and authority that is ours through the Holy Spirit over the realm of evil? **What if** we were to truly believe we have the ability to impact lives, our nation, and the world through our prayers? **What if** we were to become dead serious and committed in our prayer life? **What if** we would persist in prayer until we see the answer? **What if** we were to recognize that prayer is a declaration of both violence against and victory over Satan's domain? **What if** we grasped the truth that through prayer we can topple strongholds and demolish Satan's agenda for destruction in our lives? **What if** we were to understand that prayer is **the** most important, **the** most powerful, **the** most influential, and **the** most eternal action we could ever take?

Throughout history, God has always maintained a remnant of those who remained true to Him and adhered to His Word. They were those who endured in even the worst of times. They were those who steadfastly held onto and walked in His truth and His principles. They were those who resisted the lure of sin and worldliness. They were those whose faith prompted them to believe in His absolute power. They were those who contended to bring the Kingdom of God to Earth. They were those whose habit it was to go before the Throne of Grace. They were those whose prayers reached the ears of God. They were those who impacted their times and the future for good. They were those who birthed revival in the nations.

What if we were counted in today's remnant? *WHAT IF?* As I write the final words to this book, with tears in my eyes, a pounding heart, and trembling fingers, that is the cry of my spirit for each one of us.

Loving and gracious Father God, we come before you to worship and exalt only You. Again we acknowledge our sinfulness and ask You to forgive us. Lord, open our ears to hear the cry of the Spirit! Cause our hearts and spirits to respond to Your call! Remind us that You have intentionally placed each one of us in this time of history that we might be vessels of your glory. Remind us that this is __our watch!__ Teach us how to war in the spiritual realm. Give us courage to stand against the enemy, to take back what he has stolen from us, to push back the gates of hell! Remind us that You are the Mighty Warrior and You go before us. Remind us that You are always victorious! Stir in us a desire to pray in faith and boldness.

Father, we pray for revival across our land. We ask for You to fan the flames of faith that are growing dim and cause them to burst forth with fresh fire. We ask You to impart an insatiable hunger and thirst for Your Word and Your Spirit! We ask You to ignite hearts with a passion for You! Father, would You heal our nation and cause us to return to You?

Lord, may we respond to Your voice. May we be counted in the remnant of our time. In Jesus' Name, Amen.

PERSONAL REFLECTION

1. What is your assessment of our nation's spiritual climate?

2. What is your understanding of spiritual warfare?

3. What three **what ifs** spoke to you the most? Would you add any?

4. I pray that God has used this book, and especially the last chapter, to impress upon you, dear reader, that each one of us has our part in this battle. Each one of us is essential. I pray that God will stir in you a yearning to intercede for our nation with a new awareness and on a deeper level than perhaps you have before.

Please prayerfully consider and write down how God is asking you to respond to this chapter. Perhaps it will be in committing more time in prayer for the nation. Perhaps it will asking others to join you in that prayer. Whatever it may be, I pray we be partners in the remnant of our time, and I am looking forward to meeting you "on the other side." Imagine the stories we will have to share!

ENDNOTES

Chapter One
1. Romans 1:20.
2. Numbers 22:21-32.
3. Romans 4:17.

Chapter Two
4. Genesis 1:28.
5. Isaiah 14:12-14.
6. Revelation 12:7-9.
7. John 14:15.
8. I John 4:4.
9. Matthew 16:18.
10. I Corinthians 15:45.

Chapter Three
11. Genesis 5:24.
12. Genesis 11:10-26.
13. Genesis 12:9-19.
14. "Genesis 15 – God Confirms the Covenant with Abram," *Enduring Word,* http://www.enduringword.com/commentary/genesis15.html.
15. Genesis 17:16.
16. Genesis 17:17.
17. Genesis 17:18-19.
18. Ezekiel 16:46-52.

Chapter Four
19. Exodus 19:1.
20. Numbers 10:11.
21. Exodus 32:1.

22. Exodus 19:16.
23. Exodus 32:7-10
24. Exodus 32:11-13.
25. Numbers 12:3.
26. Numbers 14:21.
27. Exodus 32:14.
28. II Corinthians 7:10.
29. II Corinthians 3:1.
30. II Corinthians 10:13.
31. Hebrews 13:8.

Chapter Five
32. I Chronicles 15:11-25.
33. II Samuel 6:7; I Chronicles 13:9-10.
34. II Samuel 6:13.
35. II Samuel 6:20-23.
36. Exodus 33:15-16.

Chapter Six
37. II Samuel 12:13.
38. II Samuel 12:13.
39. II Samuel 12:14
40. II Timothy 3:16.
41. I Corinthians 2:16
42. II Samuel 12:18.
43. I Chronicles 28.
44. I Kings 6:37-38.
45. II Chronicles 5:3.
46. Zechariah 14:16-20.
47. II Chronicles 6:14-42.
48. I Kings 4:31.
49. II Chronicles 7:14.

Chapter Seven

50. I Kings 11:3.
51. II Kings 17:7.
52. II Kings 18:5-7.
53. Samuel Anglim, *Fighting Techniques of the Ancient World 3000 BCE-500 BCE* (Amber Books, 2013) 185-186.
54. II Kings 18:32-33.
55. Anglim, 190.
56. *Bullying,* http://www.apa.org//Home//PsychologyTopics//Bullying.
57. Matthew 5:44; Luke 6:28.
58. Zechariah 4:6

Chapter Eight

59. http//www.ids.org/manuel/old-testament-student-manual-kings-malachi-enrichment-g?lang=eng.
60. Some sources say 612 BCE as there is a difference depending on whether one is using the Babylonian calendar or the Jewish calendar.
61. www.wikipedia.org/wiki/Jewish5E2%80%Babylonianwar.
62. Again, this is due to difference in which calendar is being used.
63. Richard Gottheil, Victor Ryssel, Marcus Jastrow, Carpas Levias, "Captivity, or Exile, Babylonian" *Jewish Encyclopedia,* http://www.jewishencyclopedia.com/articles/4012-captivity.
64. http://www.bible-history.com/map-babylonian-captivity/map-of-the-deportation-ofjudah-treatment-of-the-jews-in-babylon.html.
65. Daniel 1:4.
66. http://www.gotquestions.org/Babylonianempire.html.

67. Christopher R. Smith, "Were Daniel and His Friends Eunuchs?"
http://www.goodquestionblog.com/2014/05/28/were-daniel-and-his-friends-eunchs?html.

68. *Life Application Bible, New International Version* (Grand Rapids, Michigan: Zondervan Publishing, and Wheaton, Illinois: Tyndale Publishing, 1991) 1475.

69. Daniel 6:5.

70. Daniel 6:10.

71. Daniel 9:2.

72. Jeremiah 25:11-12; 29:10.

73. Daniel 9:4-15.

74. Daniel 9:13.

75. Ezekiel 22:30

76. Psalm 50:23

77. Daniel 9:20

78. "Bible Prophecy: Daniel 9: 20-27"
http://www.amazingbible.org/documents/Bible_Prophecy/Daniel_9_11_12.htlm.

79. Psalm 119:1

80. Micah 6:8

Chapter Nine
81. For more detail refer to Jeremiah 52.

82. Isaiah 44:28.

83. *Life Application Bible, New International version* (Grand Rapids, Michigan: Zondervan Publishing, and Wheaton, Illinois: Tyndale Publishing, 1991) 772.

84. David Guzik, "David Guzik Commentary on the Bible" *Through all 66 Books of the Bible,*
http.//www.studylight.org/commentaries/guz/Nehemiah-1.html.

85. "The Babylonian Exile,"
http.//www.jewishvirtuallibrary.org/the-babylonian-exile.
86. Matthew 1 13; Luke 3:27.
87. http://en.wikipedia.org/wiki/Cup-bearer-67K.
88. Nehemiah 1:1.
89. Nehemiah 2:1.
90. Nehemiah 1:5-11.
91. The story of Joseph is found in Genesis 37, 39-50; the story of Moses is found in Exodus 2; the story of Daniel is found throughout the book of Daniel, and the story of Esther is found throughout the book of Esther.
92. Nehemiah 2:6.
93. Luke 16:10.
94. John 3:16.
95. Ezekiel 16:49-52.
96. Deuteronomy 8:12- 14.
97. Revelation 3:17.
98. Mark Batterson, *Circle Maker* (Grand Rapids, Michigan: Zondervan, 2011), 12.
99. Batterson, 12.
100. Batterson, 12.

Chapter Ten
101. Malachi 4:2-3.
102. Malachi 4:5-6.
103. Luke 1:11.
104. John 1:1-4.
105. John 1:14.
106. Dr. James Allan Francis, "One Solitary Life," *One Solitary Life – the Effect of the Life of Jesus on Mankind,* http://www.changinglives.org.au/solitary-life.html.
107. John 17:1-26.

108. I Peter 5:8.
109. John 10:10.
110. II Corinthians 10:4-5.
111. Ephesians 6:10-19.
112. Matthew 18:18
113. Ephesians 4:3
114. Matthew 12:25; Mark 3:25

Chapter Eleven
115. Luke 22:44
116. John Barnett, "Can Someone Sweat drops of Blood?" http://www. jesus.org/death-resurrection/holy-week-and-passion/can-someone-sweat-drops-of-blood.html.
117. Biblical Archaeology Staff, "Roman Crucifixion Methods reveal the History of Crucifixion", http://www.biblicalarcheology.org/daily/biblical-topics/crucifixion/roman-crucifixion-methods-reveal-the-history-of-crucifixion.html.
118. Acts 1:3.
119. II Chronicles 16:9.
120. Ezekiel 22:30.
121. Ephesians 6:10-19.
122. "Quotes on Judaism and Israel: Mark Twain," http://www.jewishvirutallibrary.org/mark-twain-quotation-on-judaism-and-israel. -1867(Quoted in Mark Twain, *The Innocents Abroad.* London: 1881) p. 361-362.

CPSIA information can be obtained
at www.ICGtesting.com
Printed in the USA
FFOW05n1443060617
36446FF